D0975524

HOW SUCCESSFUL PEOPLE WIN

Books by Dr. John C. Maxwell
Can Teach You How to Be a REAL Success

Relationships

25 Ways to Win with People
Becoming a Person of Influence
Encouragement Changes Everything
Ethics 101
Everyone Communicates, Few Connect
The Power of Partnership
Relationships 101
Winning with People

Equipping

The 15 Invaluable Laws of Growth
The 17 Essential Qualities of a Team Player
The 17 Indisputable Laws of Teamwork
Developing the Leaders Around You
How Successful People Grow
Equipping 101
Make Today Count
Mentoring 101
My Dream Map
Partners in Prayer
Put Your Dream to the Test
Learning from the Giants
Running with the Giants
Wisdom from Women in the Bible
Talent Is Never Enough
Today Matters
Your Road Map for Success

Attitude

Attitude 101
The Difference Maker
Failing Forward
How Successful People Think
Sometimes You Win—Sometimes You Learn
Sometimes You Win—Sometimes You Learn for Teens
Success 101
Thinking for a Change
The Winning Attitude

Leadership

The 5 Levels of Leadership
The 21 Irrefutable Laws of Leadership, 10th Anniversary Edition
The 21 Indispensable Qualities of a Leader
The 21 Most Powerful Minutes in a Leader's Day
The 360 Degree Leader
Developing the Leader Within You
Go for Gold
Good Leaders Ask Great Questions
How Successful People Lead
Jumpstart Your Leadership
Leadership 101
Leadership Gold
Leadership Promises for Every Day

HOW
SUCCESSFUL
PEOPLE
WIN

TURN EVERY SETBACK INTO
A STEP FORWARD

JOHN C. MAXWELL

**CENTER
STREET**

NEW YORK   BOSTON   NASHVILLE

Center Street
Hachette Book Group
1290 Avenue of the Americas
New York, NY 10104

www.CenterStreet.com

Printed in the United States of America

WOR

Originally published as *Sometimes You Win—Sometimes You Learn*
by Center Street, 2013

First edition: May 2015
10 9 8 7 6 5 4 3 2 1

Center Street is a division of Hachette Book Group, Inc.
The Center Street name and logo are trademarks of Hachette Book Group, Inc.

The Hachette Speakers Bureau provides a wide range of authors for speaking
events. To find out more, go to www.HachetteSpeakersBureau.com or
call (866) 376-6591.

The publisher is not responsible for websites (or their content) that are not owned
by the publisher.

Library of Congress Cataloging-in-Publication Data has been applied for.

*To Paul Martinelli, Scott Fay, and the thousands of
coaches around the world who are part of
the John Maxwell Team:*

You share my heart.

You communicate my values.

You live out my vision.

*You are adding value to others far beyond
my hopes and expectations.*

*Thank you for creating a legacy for me while
I'm still around to see it.*

Contents

Acknowledgments   ix

1. **What Successful People Know About Winning**   1

2. **Cultivate Humility:**
   The Spirit of Learning   11

3. **Face Reality:**
   The Foundation of Learning   21

4. **Accept Responsibility:**
   The First Step of Learning   31

5. **Seek Improvement:**
   The Focus of Learning   43

6. **Nurture Hope:**
   The Motivation of Learning   55

7. **Develop Teachability:**
   The Pathway of Learning   65

8. **Overcome Adversity:**
   The Catalyst for Learning   77

9. Expect Problems:
Opportunities for Learning   87

10. Understand Bad Experiences:
The Perspective for Learning   97

11. Embrace Change:
The Price of Learning   107

12. Benefit from Maturity:
The Value of Learning   119

**13. Winning Isn't Everything,
but Learning Is**   131

Notes   143

Acknowledgments

Thank you to:

Charlie Wetzel, my writer;

Stephanie Wetzel, my social media manager; and

Linda Eggers, my executive assistant.

HOW SUCCESSFUL PEOPLE WIN

1

What Successful People Know About Winning

My friend Robert Schuller once asked, "What would you attempt to do if you knew you wouldn't fail?" That's a great question, an inspiring question. When most people hear it, they start dreaming. They are motivated to reach for their goals and to risk more.

I have a question that I think is just as important: What do you learn when you fail? While people are usually ready to talk about their dreams, they are less prepared to answer a question about their shortcomings. Most people don't like to talk about their mistakes and failures. They don't want to confront their losses. They are embarrassed by them. And when they do find themselves falling short, they may find themselves saying something trite, such as "Sometimes you win, sometimes you lose." The message is, "Hope to win, expect to lose, and live with the results either way."

1

What's wrong with that? It's not how winners think!

Successful people know the way to turn a setback into a step forward. How? They don't try to brush failure under the rug. They don't run away from their losses. They learn from them. Every time. They understand that life's greatest lessons are gained from our losses—if we approach them the right way. Mistakes are acceptable as long as the damage isn't too great. Or as they say in Texas, "It doesn't matter how much milk you spill as long as you don't lose your cow!"

Why Losses Hurt So Much

In life, sometimes you do win. But other times you get knocked down. The key is to figure out why you got knocked down, learn from it, get back up, and move forward. That's how successful people win.

Have you ever heard someone use the phrase "It's only a game"? I bet if you have, it was from someone who was losing. Nobody likes to lose. Think of some of the losses in your life and how they made you feel. Not good. And it's not just the pain of the moment that affects us. Our losses also cause us other difficulties. Here are a few:

1. Losses Cause Us to Be Emotionally Stuck

Author and speaker Les Brown says, "The good times we put in our pocket. The bad times we put in our heart." I have found that to be true in my life. In my heart I still carry some of the bad times. I bet you do, too. The negative experiences affect us more deeply than positive ones, and if you're like me, you may get emotionally stuck. Anxiety and fear are debilitating emotions for the human heart. So are losses. They can weaken, imprison, paralyze, dishearten, and sicken us. To be successful, we need to find ways to get unstuck emotionally.

2. Losses Cause Us to Be Mentally Defeated

It cannot be denied that our lives are filled with loss. Over the course of our adult lives, we lose jobs and positions. Our self-esteem may take a beating. We lose money. We miss opportunities. Friends and family die. And I don't even want to talk about some of the physical losses we experience with advancing age! Some losses are large; some are small. And the losses we face affect our mental health. Some people handle it well, while others don't.

The quality that distinguishes a successful person from an unsuccessful one who is otherwise like him is the capacity to manage disappointment and loss. Too often losing goes to our heads. It defeats us, and we have trouble coming up with solutions to our challenges. As the losses build up, they become more of a burden. We regret the losses of yesterday. We fear the losses of tomorrow. Regret saps our energy. We can't build on regret. Fear for the future distracts us and fills us with apprehension.

We want success, but we should instead train for losses.

We need to expect mistakes, failures, and losses in life, since each of us will face many of them. But we need to take them as they come, not allow them to build up.

3. Losses Create a Gap between I Should and I Did

Winning creates a positive cycle in our lives. When we win, we gain confidence. The more confidence we have, the more likely we are to take action when it's needed. That inclination to move from knowing to acting often brings success.

However, losing can also create a cycle in our lives—a negative one. Losses, especially when they pile up, can lead to insecurity. When we are insecure, we doubt ourselves. It causes us to hesitate when making decisions. Even if we know what we should do, we are reluctant to do it. When such a gap is created and isn't overcome, success becomes nearly impossible.

Here are eleven traps that people tend to fall into:

- **The Mistake Trap:** "I'm afraid of doing something wrong." Losses hold us back.
- **The Fatigue Trap:** "I'm tired today." Losses wear us out.
- **The Comparison Trap:** "Someone else is better qualified than I am." Losses cause us to feel inferior to others.
- **The Timing Trap:** "This isn't the right time." Losses make us hesitate.

- **The Inspiration Trap:** "I don't feel like doing it right now." Losses demotivate us.
- **The Rationalization Trap:** "Maybe it's really not that important." Losses allow us to lose perspective.
- **The Perfection Trap:** "There's a best way to do it, and I have to find it before I start." Losses cause us to question ourselves.
- **The Expectation Trap:** "I thought it would be easy, but it isn't." Losses highlight the difficulties.
- **The Fairness Trap:** "I shouldn't have to be the one to do this." Losses cause us to ask, "Why me?"
- **The Public Opinion Trap:** "If I fail, what will others think?" Losses paralyze us.
- **The Self-Image Trap:** "If I fail at this, it means I am a failure." Losses negatively affect how we see ourselves.

All of these traps are caused by losses, and all of them create the gap between knowing and doing. If we want to be successful, we need to bridge that gap.

4. The First Loss Often Isn't the Biggest Loss

When we experience a loss, we have a choice. If we immediately respond to it the right way, the loss becomes smaller to us. However, if we respond the wrong way, or if we fail to respond at all, that loss becomes greater. And it often leads to other losses. As the subsequent losses come at us, they seem to become bigger and bigger, crashing over us like waves in a violent storm. As the number of losses goes up, our self-confidence goes down.

We make matters worse when we compare ourselves to others, because we rarely do so on a level playing field. We either compare our best, including our good intentions, to someone else's worst, or we compare our worst to someone else's best. That can lead to a negative cycle of self-talk. But there's something you need to know:

> The most important person you ever talk to is yourself, so be careful what you say.
> The most important person you will evaluate is yourself, so be careful what you think.
> The most important person you will love is yourself, so be careful what you do.

I believe that in times of loss, it's easy to get caught up in thinking about how we could have or should have done things differently. Our self-talk can become very negative. The more negative it becomes, the larger our losses appear to be to us. If our self-talk is angry, destructive, or guilt producing, we become even less capable of breaking free of the negative cycle.

If we can overcome an early loss and not let it become magnified, that can help us move forward. That's not always easy to do, but even someone who has faced a very great loss can learn to do it.

5. Losses Never Leave Us the Same

The number or severity of your losses isn't as important as how you experience those losses. Yes, all losses hurt. And they make an impact on us, an impact that is rarely positive. Losses change us. But we must not allow them to control us. We can't let the fear of looking silly or incompetent paralyze us. We can't let the fear of negative consequences keep us from taking risks. Allowing negative experiences of the past to warp your future is like living in a coffin. It puts a lid on you and can end your life.

How does one minimize the negative damage of debilitating losses? First, by letting them go emotionally. If we want to overcome adversity and keep from being defeated by our losses, we need to get past them. And then we need to learn from them!

Successful People Turn a Loss into a Gain

If you're going to lose—and you are because everyone does—then why not turn it into a gain? How do you do that? By learning from it. A loss isn't totally a loss if you learn something as a result of it. Your losses can come to define you if you let them. If you stay where a loss leaves you, then eventually you can get stuck there. But you can choose to change, grow, and learn from your losses.

That, of course, is not necessarily easy. A loss doesn't turn into a lesson unless we work hard to make it so. Losing gives us an opportunity to learn, but many people do not seize it. And when they don't, losing *really* hurts.

Learning is not easy during down times, because it requires us to do things that are not natural. It is hard to smile when we are not happy. It is difficult to respond positively when numb with defeat. It takes discipline to do the right thing when everything is going wrong. How can we be emotionally strong when we are emotionally exhausted? How will we face others when we are humiliated? How do we get back up when we are continually knocked down?

I wrote this book to answer these and other questions about learning from losses, because I believe it can help you win. Most of us need someone to help us figure out how to do that. If that is your desire—to become a learner from losses—you need to change the way you look at losses, cultivate qualities that help you respond to them, and develop the ability to learn from them. I believe you can do that using this road map:

Cultivate Humility: The Spirit of Learning
Face Reality: The Foundation of Learning
Accept Responsibility: The First Step of Learning
Seek Improvement: The Focus of Learning
Nurture Hope: The Motivation of Learning
Develop Teachability: The Pathway of Learning
Overcome Adversity: The Catalyst for Learning
Expect Problems: Opportunities for Learning

Understand Bad Experiences: The Perspective for
  Learning
Embrace Change: The Price of Learning
Benefit from Maturity: The Value of Learning

My primary goal in life is adding value to people. I hope
this book will add value to you, teaching you how to learn
from your losses. That's how successful people win!

2

Cultivate Humility
The Spirit of Learning

Have you noticed how easily successful people seem to bounce back from losses? They learn from them and become even better than they were before! Meanwhile, other people seem to fail, fall, and never get back up again. After they experience something negative, you can actually see the downward spiral starting. And no matter how much you want to help them, you can't. They just don't learn from their mistakes.

What is the difference between these two kinds of people? I believe it isn't due to timing, social status, the degree of adversity, or anything else outside of their control. The difference is on the inside. It's the spirit of an individual. Those who profit from adversity possess a spirit of humility and are therefore inclined to make the necessary changes needed to learn from their mistakes, failures, and losses. They stand in stark contrast to prideful people who are unwilling to allow adversity to be their teacher and as a result fail to learn.

Pride Goes before a Fall

Everyone experiences adversity. Some people are made humble by it. Others are made hard. And they carry that spirit with them everywhere they go. For those who allow themselves to become hard, that's tragic because it's very difficult for a hard person to learn anything.

Ezra Taft Benton observed, "Pride is concerned about who's right. Humility is concerned about what's right." That's a pretty accurate description. Pride causes people to justify themselves, even when they know they're wrong. And that's just the start! Take a look at the negative impact pride can have on a person:

- **Blame:** Instead of taking responsibility, prideful people blame others.
- **Denial:** Instead of being objective and realistic, they don't face reality.
- **Closed-Mindedness:** Instead of being open-minded and receptive, prideful people are defensive and opposed to new ideas.
- **Rigidity:** Instead of being flexible, prideful people are rigid.
- **Insecurity:** Prideful people inflate themselves and deflate others because they are insecure.

- **Isolation:** Instead of being connected, prideful people find themselves out of touch—with themselves, their families, their community, their clients and customers.

Do any of those descriptions apply to you? I'm sorry to say that in my formative years of leadership, I did not possess the humility needed to fill me with the spirit of learning. In fact, I was just the opposite: I was prideful, I was competitive, and I always wanted to win. And when I won, I was insufferable. If I beat someone, I told him I won. And I told everyone he knew that I had won. I put everyone on edge. What's worse is that I wasn't even aware of it. I didn't realize how unteachable I was until my friends gave me the gift of a T-shirt that read, "It's hard to be humble when you're as great as I am." Everyone laughed as they presented it to me, but internally I suspected they were trying to speak truth into my life.

Later I went to one of the presenters and asked if I really was that way.

"Yes," she said, "that's who you are. But we love you and know you can change."

That opened my eyes. Her kind words connected with me and convicted me. And I decided to try to change my attitude from expert to learner.

That decision took a long time to implement—two or three years. Arrogant people don't get humble quickly. But it was the beginning of a change in me, a desire to embrace a humility that makes learning possible. I'm still confident, but I work every day to keep that confidence from becoming a barrier to my ability to learn.

You may already be a humble person who possesses the spirit of learning. If so, that's fantastic. But if you don't, here's the good news: you can change. If I did, then you can, too. If you're not sure where you stand in regard to humility—if your friends haven't given you the T-shirt—then perhaps this can help you. Kirk Hanson, university professor and executive director of the Markkula Center for Applied Ethics at Santa Clara University, offers a list of characteristics exhibited by unteachable leaders. He says these characteristics are often the Achilles' heel of leaders. I believe they also apply to everyone who does not possess the spirit of learning. I've altered his points slightly, stating them as questions so that you can ask yourself which apply to you.

- Do you tend to believe you know it all?
- Do you tend to think you should be in charge?
- Do you sometimes believe the rules don't apply to you?
- Do you believe you shouldn't fail?
- Do you tend to believe you get things done all by yourself?
- Do you believe you are better than others with less talent or status?
- Do you think you are as important as or more important than the organization?

If you answer yes to many of these questions, you may not possess the spirit of learning. Please don't be discouraged. If you have gotten off to a bad start, don't worry. You can change. Remember, it's the finish, not the start, that counts the most in life.

How the Right Spirit Helps You Learn

Humility is foundational to all people who learn from their wins and losses. It is a key to success at the highest level.

What? you may be thinking. *I disagree! I can name a dozen people who've achieved big things with arrogant attitudes.* So can I. But what *might* they have achieved had they possessed the spirit of learning? Perhaps they would have been even greater. Humility opens the door to learning and to ever higher levels of achievement. Here's why:

1. Humility Allows Us to Possess a True Perspective of Ourselves and Life

Author and business consultant Ken Blanchard says, "Humility does not mean you think less of yourself. It means you think of yourself less." When we are focused too much on ourselves, we lose perspective. Humility allows us to regain perspective and see the big picture. It makes us realize that while we may be *in* the picture, we are not the *entire* picture.

When we possess a spirit of pride rather than humility, it clouds our view of ourselves and the world around us. When lack of humility makes us out of tune within ourselves, the world gets out of focus. We lose perspective and have difficulty learning. How can we discover our shortcomings or the things we need to learn when we can't *see* them?

Humility opens our eyes and broadens our view. Because we aren't focused on justifying ourselves or looking good, we have better judgment. Baseball great Lou Brock said, "Show me a guy who is afraid to look bad, and I'll show you a guy you can beat every time." Why? Because his eyes are closed to everything around him.

An accurate view of ourselves is difficult to obtain and even harder to keep. Humility helps.

Humility fosters an agenda of seeing things as they really are, of learning, and of the desire to improve. Where pride fosters closed-mindedness and always seeks to justify itself, humility fosters open-mindedness and a desire to improve. Humility puts things in perspective, and if we let it, it also helps us to have a better sense of humor.

2. Humility Enables Us to Learn and Grow in the Face of Losses

When people are humble enough to have a clear and realistic view of themselves, their vision is usually also clear and realistic when they face their mistakes, failures, and other losses. That ability to see clearly sets them up to learn and grow. Success lies not in eliminating our troubles and mistakes but in growing through and with them.

How does a humble person learn from mistakes? By pausing and reflecting. I strongly believe that experience isn't the best teacher; evaluated experience is. Wisely humble people are never afraid to admit they are wrong. When they do, it's as if they're saying they're wiser today than they were yesterday. And, of course, there are other side benefits. As the great American novelist Mark Twain quipped, "Always acknowledge a fault frankly. This will throw those in authority off their guard and give you an opportunity to commit more."

Mistakes can often be our best teachers. If we are willing to admit them and learn from them, we gain in knowledge and wisdom. We can do so if every time we take time to reflect on them by asking:

What went wrong?
When did it go wrong?
Where did it go wrong?
Why did it go wrong?
How did I contribute to making it go wrong?
What can I learn from this experience?
How will I apply what I've learned in the future?

Asking such questions can be a slow and uncomfortable process, especially for action-oriented people. But it always pays off. Humanity is filled with mistakes. Humility allows us to learn from them.

3. Humility Allows Us to Let Go of Perfection
and Keep Trying

My grandson John, the son of my son Joel and his wife
Liz, is a wonderful child. (I'd say that even if he weren't
my grandchild!) He's very smart, but he also tends to be
a bit serious and perfectionistic. To help him with this, his
parents bought him a book entitled *Mistakes That Worked*
by Charlotte Foltz Jones. They read through it together, and
it helps him to understand that he doesn't need to be perfect
to be successful.

In the book, Jones writes,

> Call them accidents. Call them mistakes. Even seren-
> dipity.
>
> If the truth were known, we might be amazed by
> the number of great inventions and discoveries that
> were accidental, unplanned and unintentional.
>
> The inventors mentioned in this book were not
> only smart, but also alert. It is easy to fail and then
> abandon the whole idea. It's more difficult to fail, but
> then recognize another use for the failure. . . .
>
> The inventors and discoverers mentioned in this
> book should teach all of us the lesson stated best by
> Bertolt Brecht in 1930: "Intelligence is not to make
> no mistakes. But quickly to see how to make them
> good."[1]

4. Humility Allows Us to Make the Most Out of Our Mistakes

That brings us to the final way that a humble spirit of learning helps us—by allowing us to make the most out of our mistakes and failures. When we're humble, we are open to seeing our mistakes as possibilities for innovation and success.

If you bring the right spirit to your work, you can turn a mistake into an opportunity. Success and fame don't always come to the most talented people. Sometimes they come to the person who can turn adversity into advantage. Or, as John Kenneth Galbraith says, "If all else fails, immortality can always be assured by spectacular error."

Novelist J. M. Barrie observed, "The life of every man is a diary in which he means to write one story, and writes another; and his humblest hour is when he compares the volume as it is with what he vowed to make it." That has been true for me. In many ways, I've fallen short of what I would have liked to do and be. However, in the hour when we compare what we desired to do with what we have actually done, if we are humble and open to the lessons life offers to teach us, we increase the odds of our success. And knowing that we have tried our best, perhaps we will be content with what we have been able to become and to accomplish.

3

Face Reality

The Foundation of Learning

If we want to succeed in life and to learn from our losses, we must be able to face reality and use it to create a foundation for growth. That can be very difficult. People who face horrific experiences can be crushed by them. But any loss, even a small one, can tempt us to avoid reality. We may blame other people for our circumstances. We may rationalize or make excuses. Or we may retreat into our own little world.

As much as an escape from reality may give us temporary relief from our problems, the truth is it's easier to go from failure to success than it is from excuses to success. When we lose sight of reality, we quickly lose our way. We cannot create positive change in our lives if we are confused about what's really happening. You can't improve yourself if you're kidding yourself.

Three Realities of Life

Everyone's reality is different. However, there are some realities that are true for all of life.

1. Life Is Difficult

Somehow people seem to believe that life is supposed to be easy. This is particularly a problem in America today. We expect a smooth, easy road to success. We expect our lives to be hassle free. We expect the government to solve our problems. We expect to get the prize without having to pay the price. That is not reality! Life is hard.

There is no quick and easy way. Nothing worth having in life comes without effort. That is why psychiatrist M. Scott Peck begins his book *The Road Less Traveled* with the words "Life is difficult." He wants to set the stage for everything else he communicates in the book. If we don't understand and accept the truth that life is difficult, then we set ourselves up for failure and we won't learn.

2. Life Is Difficult for Everyone

Even if we are willing to concede that life is difficult for most people, deep down inside many of us secretly hope somehow that this truth won't apply to us. I'm sorry to say it isn't so. No one escapes life's problems, failures, and losses. If we are to make progress, we must do so through life's difficulties. Or as poet Ralph Waldo Emerson stated it, "The walking of Man is falling forwards."

Life isn't easy and it isn't fair. I've had unfair things happen to me. I bet you have, too. I've made mistakes, made a fool of myself, hurt people I've loved, and experienced crushing disappointments. I bet you have, too. We cannot avoid life's difficulties. We shouldn't even try. Why? Because the people who succeed in life don't try to escape pain, loss, or unfairness. They just learn to face those things, accept them, and move ahead in the face of them. That's my goal. It should also be yours. It is how successful people win.

3. Life Is More Difficult for Some Than for Others

In a favorite *Peanuts* comic strip, the woeful Charlie Brown pours his heart out to Lucy, who is positioned in her five-cents psychiatric booth. When he tells her that he's confused about life and where he's going, she says, "Life is like a deck chair. Some people place their chairs facing the rear of the ship so they can see where they've been. Other people face their chairs forward; they want to see where they're going." Then Lucy asks, "On the cruise ship of life, Charlie Brown, which way is your deck chair facing?"

Charlie's reply: "I've never been able to get one unfolded."

Let's face it: Life is more difficult for some than it is for others. The playing field is not level. You may have faced more and greater difficulties in life than I have. You may have faced fewer. Your life right now may feel like clear sailing. Or it may feel like rough waters. And comparing our lives to others ultimately isn't that productive. Life isn't fair, and we shouldn't expect it to be. The sooner we face that reality, the better we are going to be at facing whatever is coming toward us.

Don't Make Life Harder for Yourself

Your life is probably plenty difficult already. The reality is that you will have to deal with those difficulties already no matter what. One of the keys to winning is not to make things even harder for yourself, which is, unfortunately, what many people seem to do.

To help you with this reality, I want to point out the top five ways people make life harder for themselves so that you can avoid these pitfalls.

1. Life Is More Difficult for Those Who Stop Growing and Learning

As you know, some people never make the intentional effort to grow. Some think they will grow automatically. Others don't value growth and hope to progress in life without pursuing it. For such people, life is more difficult than it would be if they were dedicating themselves to continual improvement.

People who won't grow are like the peers of the great scientist Galileo, who tried to convince them to believe what he was learning about physics. They laughed at him and refused to acknowledge his discoveries, saying that his theories could not be true because they contradicted the teachings of Aristotle.

In one instance, Galileo decided to give them a demonstration that would provide them with clear evidence of one of his observations: that two objects of different mass dropped together from the same height would reach the ground at the same time. On the day of the demonstration, the scientist climbed to the top of the Leaning Tower of Pisa. As the crowd below watched, he let drop together a ten-pound shot and a one-pound shot. They landed simultaneously. There could be no doubt that Galileo's theory was correct. Yet many still refused to believe it—in spite of the evidence they saw with their own eyes. And they continued teaching the outdated theories of Aristotle. They wanted to hold on to what they had—even though it was wrong—rather than change and grow.

While some people experience greater difficulties in life because they refuse to grow, there are additional kinds of people who create difficulties for themselves: those who become satisfied with their gains and start to plateau. Success can have a way of distorting our view of reality. It can make us think we are better than we really are. It can lure us into believing we have little left to learn. It can convince us that we should no longer expect to face and overcome failure. These are dangerous concepts to anyone who wants to keep improving.

How do we fight such ideas? By facing reality. Successful

coaches understand the importance of honest and realistic evaluation. In football, that means spending time in the film room grading the performance of the team. My friend Jim Tressel, former coach at Ohio State, says, "Grade the plays the same, win or lose." Why? Because there is a tendency to not be as objective grading plays when you win as when you lose. Winning causes people to relax and enjoy the spoils of victory. Do that and you just may coast your way to failure.

2. Life Is More Difficult for Those Who Don't Think Effectively

One of the most striking things that separate people who are successful from those who aren't is the way they think. I feel so strongly about this I wrote a book about it called *How Successful People Think*. People who get ahead think differently than those who don't. They have reasons for doing what they do, and they are continually thinking about what they're doing, why they're doing it, and how they can improve.

That doesn't mean that good thinkers always succeed. No, they make mistakes just like everyone else. But they don't keep making the *same* mistakes repeatedly. And that makes a great difference in their lives.

3. Life Is More Difficult for Those Who Don't Face Reality

Perhaps the people who have the hardest time in life are the ones who refuse to face reality.

Roots author Alex Haley observed, "Either you deal with what is the reality, or you can be sure that the reality is going to deal with you." If you want to climb the highest mountain, you can't expect to do it overnight. You can't expect to do it unless you've been trained in how to climb and gotten into physical condition. And if you try to deny reality and make the climb anyway, you're going to end up in trouble.

What you do matters. And to be successful, what you do must be based on reality. Journalist Sydney J. Harris observed, "An idealist believes the short run doesn't count. A cynic believes the long run doesn't matter. A realist believes that what is done or left undone in the short run determines the long run."

Life is difficult. But here's the good news: many of the things you desire to do in life are attainable—if you are willing to face reality, know your starting place, count the cost of your goal, and put in the work. Don't let your real situation discourage you. Everyone who got where they are started where they were.

4. Life Is More Difficult for Those Who Are Slow to Make Proper Adjustments

My older brother, Larry, has been a mentor to me in many areas. He is especially gifted when it comes to business and finance. Often I have heard him say, "People don't cut their losses quickly enough." He has taught me to make my first loss my last loss. I find that difficult to do. Do you? Instead of cutting our losses, we rationalize. We try to defend the decision. We wait to see if it will change and prove us right. Larry advised me to face up to a problem and either fix it or bail out.

The great heavyweight boxer Evander Holyfield said, "Everyone has a plan until they are hit." What did he mean by that? The stress of a difficult situation can make you forget your plan, and if you don't handle the situation well, you won't be able to make adjustments. Yet that is exactly what you need to be able to do to be successful—make good adjustments.

While it's true that acceptance of a problem does not conquer it, if you face reality you create a foundation that makes it possible for you to make proper adjustments. And that greatly increases your odds of success.

5. Life Is More Difficult for Those Who Don't Respond Correctly to Challenges

People who respond correctly to adversity realize that their response to a challenge is what impacts the outcome. They accept and acknowledge the reality of their situation, and then act accordingly. I didn't find that to be easy at first. My natural optimism tends to make me want to ignore a crisis and hope it will go away. That doesn't work. Wishing isn't solving.

Denying a problem only makes it worse. So does getting angry and yelling, or taking it out on loved ones. I had to learn to say to myself, "This is the way it is. I have a problem. If I want to solve it, I need to take action. What is the best solution?" When you have a challenge, you can turn lemons into lemonade, or you can let them sour your whole life. It's your choice.

Facing reality, maintaining a confident sense of expectation, and performing at your best may not be easy, but it is possible. And it does make a huge difference in your life. It sets you up to learn, to grow, and to succeed. You create opportunities by looking trouble in the eye and performing, not looking away and pretending. If you want to learn, you must build your problem solving, your planning, and your performance on a solid foundation. Reality is the only thing that won't crumble under the weight of those things.

4

Accept Responsibility
The First Step of Learning

We tend to think of responsibility as something *given* to us by someone who is in a position of authority, such as a parent or an employer. And that is often the case. But responsibility is also something we must be willing to *take*. And after more than forty-five years leading and mentoring people, I have come to the conclusion that responsibility is the most important ability that a person can possess. Nothing happens to advance our potential until we step up and say, "I am responsible." If you don't take responsibility, you give up control of your life.

Taking responsibility for your life, your actions, your mistakes, and your growth puts you in a place where you are always able to learn and often able to win. In sports, that's called being in the right position. When players put themselves in the right position, they are able to successfully play. It's not a guarantee that they will make a play or that they will win. However, if they are out of position, it is almost impossible for them to make a play. Miss enough plays, and you lose the game.

Every time we fail, we can choose to put ourselves in the painful but potentially profitable place of taking responsibility so that we can take right actions for our success, or we can avoid the temporary pain of responsibility and make excuses. If we respond right to failure by taking responsibility, we can look at our failure and learn from it. As a result, we won't be as prone to making the same mistake again. However, if we bail out on our responsibility, we don't examine our failures and don't learn from them. As a result, we often experience the same failures and losses repeatedly over time. When that happens, we can't win.

What Happens When We Don't Take Responsibility

People avoid responsibility all the time, especially when they fail or make mistakes. They just don't want to face up to those things. If we do that long enough, a pattern begins to emerge in our lives:

1. We Develop a Victim Mentality

Rather than taking responsibility for their lives, many people are trying to take the easy way out by establishing themselves as victims of society, the economy, a conspiracy, or some alleged discrimination. A victim mind-set causes people to focus on what they cannot do instead of what they can do. It is a recipe for continued failure.

How do we avoid that fate? By developing gratitude for what we do have and taking responsibility. Do those things and our lives can begin to turn around.

2. We Have an Unrealistic Perspective of How Life Works

Life doesn't always work the way we'd like it to. If we had our way, it would be easier. It would be fair. It would be more fun. There'd be no pain and suffering. We would have to work only if we felt like it. And we would never die. But that isn't how life works. Life isn't easy. It's not fair. We do experience pain. Even the best of jobs includes unpleasant tasks and has times of drudgery. And every one of us will die.

Is that fair? No. Life isn't fair. In life, we all get better than we deserve at times and worse than we deserve at others. And there is no guarantee that it will balance out in the end. We can get stuck asking why. But seeking answers to that question rarely helps. We may never know why things happen. If we focus on the why, we may never make real progress in our lives.

Another pitfall is comparing ourselves to others. That can lead to tremendous frustration and dissatisfaction, because you can always find someone better off than you are.

Benjamin Franklin wrote, "Those things that hurt, instruct." That's true, but only if you make an effort to understand how life works and accept it. Instead of focusing on *why* things happen, we are better off learning *how* things work. There are more lessons to be learned, and those lessons prepare us for future battles.

3. We Constantly Engage in "Blamestorming"

Another pattern that people fall into when they don't take responsibility is what I call "blamestorming." That's the creative process used for finding an appropriate scapegoat. One time I was counseling a man who had made a mess of his life and relationships. As we got started in the process of working on his issues, he told me, "There are three things wrong with me: my wife, my mother, and my son." Now that's blamestorming.

It's my understanding that insurance companies are the recipients of many creative excuses from drivers who refuse to take responsibility for themselves. I enjoy reading these kinds of things, and I hope you will, too. Here are some of my favorites:

"As I reached the intersection, a hedge sprang up, obscuring my vision."

"An invisible car came out of nowhere, struck my car, and vanished."

"The telephone pole was approaching fast. I attempted to swerve out of its path when it struck my front end."

"The indirect cause of this accident was a little guy in a small car with a big mouth."

"I had been driving my car for four years when I fell asleep at the wheel and had an accident."

"I was on my way to the doctor's with rear end trouble when my universal joint gave way, causing me to have an accident."

"To avoid hitting the bumper of the car in front of me, I struck the pedestrian."

Any form of blamestorming may be handy in the moment, but it's not helpful in the long run. You can't grow and learn if your focus is on finding someone else to blame instead of looking at your own shortcomings.

4. We Give Away the Choice to Control Our Lives

Who is responsible for what happens in your life? Do you believe you should take personal responsibility? Or do you feel as if that is outside of your control and there's little or nothing you can do about it?

Psychologists say that some people possess an *internal* locus of control, where they rely primarily on themselves for the gains and losses in their lives. Others possess an *external* locus of control, where they blame others when something goes wrong. Which group is more successful? The group that takes personal responsibility. Which people are more content? The ones who take personal responsibility. Which people learn from their mistakes and keep growing and improving? The people who take responsibility.

Taking responsibility for your life is a choice. That doesn't mean you believe you are in control of everything in your life. That's not humanly possible. But you can take responsibility for yourself and every choice you have.

Abolitionist Henry Ward Beecher asserted, "God asks no man whether he will accept life. That is not a choice. You must take it. The only choice is how." How will you approach your life? Will you simply allow life to happen to you? Or will you seize the choices you make with enthusiasm and responsibility?

5. We Eliminate Any Possibility of Growth for Success

When we fail to take responsibility, not only do we develop a victim mentality, embrace an unrealistic perspective of how life works, engage in blamestorming, and give away the choice to control our lives, but we also eliminate any real possibility of growth for success. And that is the real tragedy of failing to be responsible.

Real success is a journey. We have to approach it with a long-term mind-set. We have to hang in there, stay focused, and keep moving forward. Excuses are like exits along the road of success that lead us nowhere. Taking the exit is easy, but it gets us off track. It is impossible to go from excuses to success. So we need to get back on the road and keep moving forward. If we want to do something and we take responsibility, we'll find a way. If not, we'll find an excuse. That may take the pressure off of us and make us feel better in the short term, but in the long run it won't make us successful.

Richard Bach said, "Argue for your limitations, and sure enough, they are yours." I may not like it, but I am responsible for who I am and where I am today. My present circumstances are a direct result of my past choices. My future will be the result of my current thoughts and actions. I am responsible, and so are you.

What Happens When We Learn to Be Responsible?

In *You Gotta Keep Dancin'*, Tim Hansel says, "Pain is inevitable, but misery is optional." A similar thing can be said when it comes to taking responsibility. Losses are inevitable, but excuses are optional. When we move from excuses to responsibility, our lives begin to change dramatically. Here's how.

1. We Take Our First Step in Learning

When you take responsibility for yourself, you take responsibility for your learning. The earlier you do this, the better the potential results.

If you take responsibility when you're young, you have a better chance of gaining wisdom as you get older. For some of us, it takes a long time. I sometimes feel that only after turning sixty-five did I begin to understand life. Now that I'm officially a senior citizen, I can say there are two things I know about my life. First, it has contained many surprises. My life didn't turn out as I thought it would. Some things turned out better than I imagined, some things worse. No matter who you are, it's impossible to know how your life will turn out.

Second, as long as I take responsibility for the things I can control in my life and try my best to learn from them, I can feel contented. Unfortunately, my personal challenge has been keeping myself from trying to control things outside my sphere of influence. Whenever I've overreached in that way and things have gone wrong, it has caused me to lose focus, waste energy, and feel discouraged. That has been a hard lesson for me.

If you can find the right balance where you take responsibility for the things you can control and let go of the things you cannot, you will accelerate your learning process. But even if you learn the lesson late, you can still benefit from it.

2. We See Things in Their Proper Perspective

Taking responsibility for yourself does not mean taking yourself too seriously. When you do that, it carries over into a negative perspective in other areas of your life. Taking responsibility doesn't mean cultivating a negative attitude. It means being willing to see things from a better perspective.

I've met people who allow their losses to overwhelm them. They say things like "That incident ruined my life" or "That person makes me so mad." The truth is that nothing can ruin your life or make you mad without your permission! If you find yourself thinking along those lines, stop immediately. You have the power to choose another way of thinking, and you can learn how to do that by maintaining a proper perspective.

The best learners are people who don't see their losses and failures as permanent. They see them as temporary. Or as Patricia Sellers once put it, "The most successful [people] at bouncing back view failure not like a cancer but, rather, like puberty: awkward and uncomfortable, but a transforming experience that precedes maturity."[2]

3. We Stop Repeating Our Failures

What's the major difference between people who succeed and people who don't? It's not failing. Both groups fail. However, the ones who take responsibility for themselves learn from their failures and *do not repeat them*.

If you think about it, how did you learn to walk when you were a baby? You tried something that didn't work and fell down. Then you tried something else that didn't work, and fell down. You probably tried *hundreds* of approaches—maybe thousands—all of which taught you what *didn't* work when it came to walking. And finally, you tried something that *did* work.

That's the way you learned to walk, eat, talk, ride a bike, throw a ball, and all the other basic tasks of living. Why would you think you'll ever get to a place where you can learn without failing and making mistakes? If you want to learn more, you need to do more. But you also need to pay attention to what's *not* working and make adjustments accordingly.

Failure isn't the best teacher. Neither is experience. Only evaluated experience teaches us. That's where the profit lies in any experience we have. That's what helps us to learn and ultimately to win.

4. We Grow Stronger

Eleanor Roosevelt observed, "You gain strength, courage, and confidence by every experience in which you really stop to look fear in the face. You are able to say to yourself, 'I have lived through this horror. I can take the next thing that comes along.' You must do the thing you think you cannot do."

Every time that you take responsibility, face your fear, and move forward despite experiencing losses, failures, mistakes, and disappointments, you become stronger. And if you keep doing the things you ought to do when you ought to do them, the day will come when you will get to do the things you want to do when you want to do them.

5. We Back Up Our Words with Our Behavior

The ultimate step in taking responsibility is making sure our actions line up with our words. If you are willing to put your name on anything you do, that indicates a high level of integrity. To put your life on the line indicates an even higher one.

That's what author and consultant Frances Cole Jones describes in her book *The Wow Factor*. She writes,

> In the Marines, "riggers"—the people who pack (i.e., reassemble after use) parachutes for other Marines—have to make at least one jump a month. Who packed their 'chute? They do: One of the parachutes that *they* packed for others to use is chosen at random, and the rigger has to "jump it." This system helps make sure that no one gets sloppy—after all, "The chute you're packing may be your own."
>
> The Roman army used a similar technique to make sure bridges and aqueducts were safe: The person who designed the arches had to stand under each arch while the scaffolding was being removed.
>
> If you want your company to last as long as Roman bridges have, ask yourself if everyone is *truly* responsible for outcomes by these measures—and

if you yourself are. Are you performing every task with the concentration and commitment that you might if a life depended on it?[3]

It may sound like hyperbole when Jones asks if you are taking responsibility for the tasks you perform as if your life depends on it, but it's not really extreme. Why? Because our lives *do* depend on what we do. The life we have is the only life we get here on earth, and it's not a dress rehearsal. Every minute we waste is gone forever. We can either choose to take responsibility for what we do with it, or we can make excuses.

I hope, like me, you are choosing to face reality and take responsibility. If you do that, then you will be ready to dig in and focus on improvement, which is the subject of the next chapter.

5

Seek Improvement

The Focus of Learning

Most of us don't expect to achieve perfection. But we do want to perform at a higher level. That requires improvement. It's been said that the three most difficult words to say are "I was wrong." When we make a mistake or fail, we don't want to admit it. Instead, we often do one of the following:

- **Blow Up:** We react with anger, resentment, blame, rationalization, and compensation.
- **Cover Up:** We try to hide our mistakes to protect our image and ourselves. A person who makes a mistake and then offers an excuse for it has made two mistakes.
- **Back Up:** We withdraw and begin distancing ourselves from those who might discover our mistake.

• **Give Up:** We throw up our hands and quit. We never address the mistake in a healthy way.

For example, John H. Holliday, who was the founder and editor of the *Indianapolis News*, stormed into the composing room one day, determined to find the culprit who had spelled *height* as *hight*. A check of the original copy indicated that he himself had been the one responsible for the misspelling. When he was told that, he said, "Well, if that's the way I spelled it, that has to be right." For the next thirty years, the *Indianapolis News* misspelled the word *height*.

Insights on Improvement

The Stone Age didn't end because people ran out of stones. It ended because people kept learning and improving. The desire to improve themselves is in the DNA of all successful people. Getting better has been a personal passion with me for many years. Part of that involves striving to perform better day by day, but the desire for improvement has also prompted me to study others who share this passion. That has helped me to learn some important things when it comes to improvement, which I want to pass along to you.

1. Improving Yourself Is the First Step to Improving Everything Else

A few years ago I was leading a roundtable of twenty highly successful people. One man expressed his frustration at having plateaued in his business and personal life. He asked, "How can I keep from plateauing?" As we asked questions and he opened up, we made a discovery. He was more concerned about his personal success than he was his personal growth. That was getting in his way.

Success does not always bring growth, but personal growth will always add to our success. The highest reward for our toil is not what we get *for* it but what we become *by* it. The most important question is not "What am I getting?" but "What am I becoming?"

The world is moving along at an incredible pace. I joked earlier about the end of the Stone Age. Some archaeologists believe that period lasted millions of years. The Bronze Age, which followed it, lasted roughly two thousand years. The Iron Age, which came next, was less than a thousand years. Each period in technological history has come faster and faster.

In the modern era, knowledge, technology, and improvements continue to accelerate. Now that we live in the information age, the world is moving even faster. Economists at UC Berkeley recently calculated that in the year 2000, the total amount of information produced worldwide was the equivalent of 37,000 times as much information as the entire holdings in the Library of Congress. In 2003, the amount of new information created was more than double that.[4] And those numbers came from the time before Twitter, Facebook, YouTube, and other information-generating options were available.

The bottom line is clear. If you are not moving forward, the world is passing you by. If you want to improve your life, your family, your work, your economic situation, your influence, or anything else, you need to first improve yourself.

2. Improvement Requires Us to Move Out of Our Comfort Zone

Novelist Fyodor Dostoyevsky observed, "Taking a new step, uttering a new word, is what people fear most." Instead people should most fear the opposite—not taking the step. Why? Because if we don't step forward out of our comfort zone and into the unknown, we will not improve and grow. Security does not take us forward. It does not help us to overcome obstacles. It does not lead to progress. You'll never get anywhere interesting if you always do the safe thing. You must surrender security to improve.

What does it take to get us to move out of our comfort zone? In my observation, it requires two things:

Handling Our Aversion to Making Mistakes

We need to fail quickly so that we can get it out of the way. If we're not failing or making mistakes, it means we're playing it too safe. Management expert Peter Drucker explained, "I would never promote a person into a high-level job who was not making mistakes.... Otherwise he is sure to be mediocre."

Mistakes are not failures. They are proof that we are making an effort. When we understand that, we can more easily move out of our comfort zone, try something new, and improve.

OVERCOMING A LIFE CONTROLLED BY FEELINGS

Improvement demands a commitment to grow long after the mood in which it was made has passed. Speaker Peter Lowe once told me, "The most common trait I have found in successful people is that they conquered the temptation to give up." Not being controlled by our feelings means that we can face our fears, get out of our comfort zone, and try new things. That is an important part of innovation.

3. Improvement Is Not Satisfied with "Quick Fixes"

We live in a society with destination disease. Too many people want to do enough to "arrive," and then they want to retire. Losers don't lose because they focus on losing. They lose because they focus on just getting by.

Improvement doesn't come to people who fixate on quick fixes. It comes to the slow but steady people who keep working at getting better. If you have a quick fix mind-set, then you need to shift it to continuous improvement. That means doing two things:

Accept the Fact That Improvement Is a Never-Ending Battle

I believe all of us can identify with the poet Carl Sandberg, who said, "There is an eagle in me that wants to soar and a hippopotamus in me that wants to wallow in the mud." The key to success is following the impulse to soar more than the desire to wallow. And that is a never-ending struggle—at least it has been for me. I believe any successful person would be honest in saying, "I got to the top the hard way—fighting my own laziness and ignorance every step of the way."

If you are just beginning your improvement journey, don't be discouraged. Your starting point doesn't matter. Everyone who has gotten to where he is started where he was. What matters is where you end up. And you get there by continuing to fight the improvement battle. As you do, make this your motto:

I'm not where I'm supposed to be,
I'm not what I want to be,
But I'm not what I used to be.
I haven't learned how to arrive;
I've just learned how to keep on going.

If you can live those words, you will eventually be successful.

Accept the Fact That Improvement
Is a Result of Small Steps

People today are looking for a secret to success. They want a magic bullet, an easy answer, a single thing that will catapult them to fortune or fame. Success generally doesn't work that way. As Andrew Wood observed, "Success in most things comes not from some gigantic stroke of fate, but from simple, incremental progress." That's pretty boring, isn't it? It may not be exciting, but it is true. Small differences over time create a big difference! Improvement is achieved in inches, not giant leaps.

Writer and artist Elbert Hubbard observed, "The line between failure and success is so fine that we scarcely know when we pass it—so fine that we are often on the line and we do not know it. How many a man has thrown up his hands at a time when a little more effort, a little more patience, would have achieved success?" That's why we need to dedicate ourselves to small steps of improvement. Who knows if the next small step will provide the breakthrough we've been seeking?

4. Improvement Is a Daily Commitment

Some things simply have to be done every day. You know the old saying "An apple a day keeps the doctor away"? Well, eating seven apples all at once isn't going to give you the same benefit. If you want to improve, intentional growth needs to be a habit. A habit is something you do continually, not once in a while. Motivation may get you going, but the positive habits you develop and practice consistently are what keep you improving.

As I have worked to improve on a day-by-day basis, two words have helped me to stay on track. The first is *intention*. Every morning as I start my day, I intend to learn something that day. This develops a mind-set in me to look for things that will help me improve.

The other word is *contemplation*. Time alone is essential for self-improvement. When I spend time thinking about my challenges, experiences, and observations, it allows me to gain perspective. I can evaluate any losses and I can learn from them. Contemplation time by myself also gives me time to do positive self-talk. Motivational humorist Al Walker stated, "The most important words we will ever utter are those words we say to ourselves, about ourselves, when we are by ourselves." During these "conversations" we can beat ourselves up and make ourselves feel really small, or we can learn and build ourselves up so that we become better.

If you want to spend some time each day to try to improve yourself, you may want to begin by asking yourself these three questions at the end of the day, as I do:

- **What did I learn today?** What spoke both to my heart and my head?

- **How did I grow today?** What touched my heart and affected my actions?
- **What will I do differently?** Unless I can state specifically what I plan to do differently, I won't learn anything.

One of the things I *don't* do is compare myself to others during that time. There's a reason for that. My desire is to not become superior to anybody else. I only want to be superior to my former self. Intention and contemplation assist me in doing that.

Make Improvement Intentional

Improvement is within the reach of anyone, no matter how experienced or green, educated or ignorant, rich or poor. To start improving today, do these three things:

1. Decide You Are Worth Improving

To improve yourself, you must believe you can improve. You can invest in yourself. You don't need anyone's dreams but your own. And you don't need to become anyone other than yourself at your best. The great philosopher Thomas Carlyle once wrote, "Let each become all that he was created capable of being." I can't think of a better definition of success. Life challenges us every day to develop our capabilities to the fullest. We're successful when we reach for the highest that's within us—when we give the best we have. Life doesn't require us to always come out on top. It asks only that we do our best to improve at whatever level of experience we are currently on.

2. Pick an Area to Improve

Most of us either want to improve nothing, or we are so impatient to become all that we can that we try to improve all that we are at the same time. Those are both mistakes. We need to focus. Noted psychologist William Jones advised, "If you would be rich, you will be rich; if you would be good, you will be good; if you would be learned, you will be learned. But wish for one thing exclusively, and don't at the same time wish for a hundred other incompatible things just as strongly."

You will have plenty of time to improve other areas of your life. Focus on the one now that makes the most of your strengths and is closest to your sense of purpose. Take the advice of Earl Nightingale, who suggested spending an hour a day improving in that area. Then take it slow but steady. We always overestimate what we can get done in a day or a week. But we underestimate what we can get done in a year. Just imagine what you will be able to get done in five years.

3. Find Opportunities to Improve in the Wake of Your Losses

Focused, strategic improvement is important to success. But so is learning from our losses as they come. I will address that more specifically in the chapters on adversity, problems, and bad experiences. However, let me say this: Some lessons in life cannot wait. You must make the most of them when they occur. If you don't examine what went wrong while the details are fresh, you may lose the ability to learn the lesson. Besides, if you neglect to learn the lesson immediately, you may experience the loss again! Knowledge may come from study, but wisdom comes from learning and improving in the wake of your mistakes.

I always try to remember that I am a work in progress. When I maintain that perspective, I realize that I don't have to be perfect. I don't have to have it all together. I don't need to try to have all the answers. And I don't need to learn everything in a day. When I make a mistake, it's not because I'm a failure or worthless. I just didn't do something right because I still haven't improved enough in some part of the process. And that motivates me to keep growing and improving. If I don't know something, it's an opportunity to try to improve in a new area.

I'm in it for the long haul. I try to be like industrialist Ian MacGregor, who said, "I work on the same principle as people who train horses. You start with low fences, easily achieved goals, and work up." When I got started, my fences were embarrassingly low. But in time I was able to raise them. Today, I'm still raising them little by little. That's the only way I know how to keep improving, and I always want to keep doing that, because improvement is the focus of learning.

6

Nurture Hope

The Motivation of Learning

As you may know, leadership is one of my passions. I learn about it every day, and it is one of my great joys to teach it to others. Former Cabinet member John W. Gardner said, "The first and last task of a leader is to keep hope alive—the hope that we can finally find our way through to a better world—despite the day's action, despite our own inertness, shallowness, and wavering resolve." The great general Napoleon said even more simply: "Leaders are dealers in hope."

As a leader and writer, I want to be someone who gives others hope. I believe that if a leader helps people believe the impossible is possible, it makes the impossible probable. So as you read this chapter, regardless of what losses you face or difficulties you must overcome, keep your head up.

Losses in life are never fun, but there is one loss no one can afford to experience—the loss of hope. If you lose hope, that may be your last loss, because when hope is gone, so is motivation and the ability to learn.

Hope Is a Beautiful Thing

In 1979 I wrote my first book, *Think on These Things*. It grew out of my desire to help people think upon the things that would build up their lives. One chapter was on the subject of hope. In it, I wrote the following words:

What does hope do for mankind?

- Hope shines brightest when the hour is darkest.
- Hope motivates when discouragement comes.
- Hope energizes when the body is tired.
- Hope sweetens when the bitterness bites.
- Hope sings when all melodies are gone.
- Hope believes when the evidence is limited.
- Hope listens for answers when no one is talking.
- Hope climbs over obstacles when no one is helping.
- Hope endures hardship when no one is caring.
- Hope smiles confidently when no one is laughing.
- Hope reaches for answers when no one is asking.
- Hope presses toward victory when no one is encouraging.
- Hope dares to give when no one is sharing.
- Hope brings the victory when no one is winning.

In short, hope gives. It gives to us even when we have little or nothing left. It is one of the most precious things we have in life.

Hope is inspiring. It gives us the motivation for living and learning. I say that for several reasons:

1. Hope Says Yes to Life

Shortly before he died, author and theologian Paul Tillich was asked about the central theme of his book *The Courage to Be*. Tillich said the book was about real courage: saying yes to life in spite of all the hardship and pain which are part of human existence. It takes courage to find something positive and meaningful about ourselves and life every day. That, he said, was the key to living life more fully. "Loving life," he stated, "is perhaps the highest form of the courage to be."

Where does a person find the courage to say yes to life? I believe it comes from hope. In life, you must expect trouble. You must expect adversity. You must expect conflict. But those facts don't mean you have to lose hope. You can take the advice of Ann Landers, who said, "Expect trouble as an inevitable part of life and when it comes, hold your head high, look it squarely in the eye, and say, 'I will be bigger than you. You cannot defeat me.'"

2. Hope Fills Us with Energy

It's been said that a person can live forty days without food, four days without water, four minutes without air, but only four seconds without hope. Why? Hope provides the power that energizes us with life. Hope is a powerful thing. It keeps us going when times are tough. It creates excitement in us for the future. It gives us reasons to live. It gives us strength and courage.

I think it's no coincidence that people who suffer with depression often lack energy. Lack of hope and lack of energy usually go hand in hand. People who have a hard time believing in themselves have a difficult time finding the energy to cope with life and its challenges. In contrast, hope-filled people are energetic. They welcome life and all that it brings—even its challenges.

3. Hope Focuses Forward

Our yesterdays have a tendency to invade our todays with negativism, stealing our joy and hope. If we dwell on them too much, they threaten to rob us of our future. That's why I like these words of Ralph Waldo Emerson: "Finish each day and be done with it.... You have done what you could; some blunders and absurdities no doubt crept in; forget them as soon as you can. Tomorrow is a new day; you shall begin it well and serenely."

Hope always has a future. It leans forward with expectation. It desires to plan for tomorrow. And that opens us up to greater possibilities.

Are you looking forward? Do you have hope for the future? If you have high expectations for tomorrow, then you probably want to meet it at your best. How do you do that? By growing, learning, and improving. Lack of hope breeds indifference toward the future. Hope brings motivation.

4. Hope Is a Difference Maker

Hope is our greatest asset and the greatest weapon we can use to battle our losses when they seem to be mounting. It is powerful, and that is why I call it a difference maker. What does hope do for us?

- Hope looks for the lesson in defeat instead of just leaving you feeling defeated.
- Hope discovers what *can* be done instead of what *can't* be done.
- Hope regards problems, small or little, as opportunities.
- Hope lights a candle instead of cursing the darkness.
- Hope opens doors where despair closes them.
- Hope draws its strength from *what can be* instead of *what was.*
- Hope cherishes no illusions nor does it yield to cynicism.
- With hope, failure is a skipping stone. Without hope, failure is a tombstone.

If you want to find the motivation to learn in the face of your losses, to keep working to get better tomorrow than you are today, to reach your potential and fulfill your purpose, then make use of the difference maker. Embrace hope.

How to Cultivate Hope

Since hope is such a beautiful thing, this question has to be asked: "Can *anyone* have it?" The answer is yes! Regardless of your present situation, background, personality, upbringing, or circumstances, you can be a person of hope. Doing the following three things will help you to get there:

1. Realize That Hope Is a Choice

Hope is in the DNA of successful men and women who learn from their losses. When times are tough, they choose hope, knowing that it will motivate them to learn and turn them from victims into victors.

Some people say choosing hope is a pie-in-the-sky approach to life. It's unrealistic, they claim. I disagree. In *The Dignity of Difference*, Jonathan Sacks writes, "One of the most important distinctions I have learned in the course of reflection on Jewish history is the difference between *optimism* and *hope*. Optimism is the belief that things will get better. Hope is the faith that, together, we can make things better. Optimism is a passive virtue, hope an active one. It takes no courage to be an optimist, but it takes a great deal of courage to have hope."[5]

I believe everyone is capable of choosing hope. Does it

take courage? Yes. Because hope can be disappointing. But I am convinced that the courage of choosing hope is always rewarded.

2. Change Your Thinking

In general we get what we expect in life. I don't know why that is true, but it is. Norman Cousins remarked, "The main trouble with despair is that it is self-fulfilling. People who fear the worst tend to invite it. Heads that are down can't scan the horizon for new openings. Bursts of energy do not spring from a spirit of defeat. Ultimately, helplessness leads to hope-lessness." If your expectations for life are negative, you end up experiencing a lot of negatives. And those negatives are compounded and become especially painful, because nega-tive expectations cause a person not to learn from their losses.

The good news is that you don't have to live with it. You can change your thinking from a negative mind-set, in which you feel hopeless, don't learn from your losses, and are tempted to give up, to a positive mind-set, in which you believe things can get better, you learn from your mistakes, and you never quit.

People give up because they lose hope. Their thinking is negative, their expectations are low, and they don't know how to get out of that pattern. The answer may not be easy, but it is simple. They need to change the way they think about themselves and the losses they experience. In life, we see what we are prepared to see. That is a result of our thinking. What we see is what we get. And that determines the outcome in much of what we do.

My favorite baseball hitter of all time was Tony Gwynn, who played for the Padres when I lived in San Diego. Year after year he led the league in batting average. One time I attended a game with a friend of Tony's. As we sat watching the game, Tony came up to bat and I said to Tony's friend, "I love to watch him hit. Why do you think he's so successful?"

"He expects to get a hit every time he bats," the friend replied.

Did Tony *always* get a hit? Of course not. That's impossible. The greatest hitters of all time fail six times out of ten. But those misses did not determine his expectation. He always believed in himself and his ability to get a hit. We should imitate him, because too often our main limitation comes from our expectations.

It's simple, but it's not easy. If you have been a negative thinker whose motivation has been rarely fueled by hope, then you must make a determination every day to try to renew your hope, change your thinking for the better, and believe that good things can and will happen to you. Doing these things can literally change your life.

3. Win Some Small Victories

If you are able to tap into your hope and become more positive in your thinking, that's a great start. But it's not enough.

Positive thinking must be followed by positive doing. If you want to succeed big, then start by trying for a small victory. Nothing encourages hope like success.

If you are able to win small victories, it encourages you. It raises your morale. When you experience a win once, you begin to understand how it works. You get better at succeeding, and after winning several victories you begin to sense that bigger victories are nearly within your grasp.

Creating a positive environment with positive experiences can go a long way to encourage you to keep hoping, keep trying, and keep learning.

7

Develop Teachability
The Pathway of Learning

People often ask me what most determines if they will reach their potential. My answer: a teachable spirit.

What does it mean to be teachable? I define *teachability* as possessing the intentional attitude and behavior to keep learning and growing throughout life. Some people don't have that. Some people want to be right, even when they aren't. And as a result, life is difficult for them. They never find the pathway of learning, nor do they learn the lessons life offers to those with a teachable spirit. Such people find it difficult to win or find success.

Even if you do know something well, it won't do everything for you. Living to your potential requires you to keep learning and expanding yourself. For that, you must have a teachable spirit. If you don't, you will come to the end of your potential long before you come to the end of your life.

If you want to be successful tomorrow, then you must be teachable today. What got you to where you are won't keep you there. And it certainly won't take you where you want to go. You need more than a great mind for learning. You need to have a great *heart* for learning. That's what a teachable spirit gives you.

We choose whether we are open or closed to new ideas, new experiences, others' ideas, people's feedback, and a willingness to change. We can choose the pathway to a better future by developing a teachable spirit, or we can sabotage that future by pretending that we know everything we need to move forward in life—which, by the way, is impossible for *anyone*!

Traits of a Teachable Person

If you desire to find the pathway from failure to success, you need to become a highly teachable person. How do you do that? By cultivating the following five traits:

1. Teachable People Have an Attitude Conducive to Learning

People with a teachable spirit approach each day as an opportunity for another learning experience. Their hearts are open. Their minds are alert for something new. Their attitudes are expectant. They know that success has less to do with possessing natural talent and more to do with choosing to learn.

When we are young, parents, teachers, and the educational system take primary responsibility for our learning. But that external impetus and responsibility for us to learn is gradually withdrawn over the course of our educational career. As we get older, and especially when we enter middle school and then move beyond it, a dividing line starts to appear between those who continue to be teachable and those who resist learning. The choice we make at that time is significant. We can choose to remain teachable and fuel our internal desire to intentionally grow. Or we can become indifferent to the opportunities that present themselves for us to keep learning.

Being teachable depends on two things: capacity and attitude. Our capacity may to some degree be set. But our attitude is totally our choice. We must proactively decide to embrace an attitude of teachability. Only rarely have I known a teachable person whose approach toward life was negative. Most people with a teachable spirit and positive attitude don't allow negative ideas to hijack their thinking. Why? A closed mind does not open doors of opportunity. A scarcity mind-set seldom creates abundance. A negative attitude rarely creates positive change.

If you have not cultivated a positive attitude and teachable spirit, I encourage you to fight for them. The sooner you do it, the better, because as age increases, our negative thoughts, bad habits, and weak character traits become more permanently ingrained. Getting older doesn't mean getting better. It just means you have less time in which to make the choice to become teachable. So make the choice to be teachable now. I know of no other way to keep learning in life.

2. Teachable People Possess a Beginner's Mind-set

Successful people are continually learning new things. What's the best way to do that? Have a beginner's mind-set. If you want to grow and learn, you must approach as many things as you can as a beginner, not an expert.

What do all beginners have in common? They know they don't know it all, and that shapes the way they approach things. In general, they're open and humble, lacking in the rigidity that often accompanies achievement.

Most people enjoy being experts. In fact, some enjoy it so much and feel so uncomfortable as beginners that they work hard to avoid putting themselves in those situations. Others are more open and enjoy learning something new. When they are actually beginners, they find it easy to have a beginner's mind-set. But maintaining that teachability becomes more difficult as you learn more and achieve some degree of success. It's a challenge to remain receptive and open in every circumstance and situation over the course of time.

I try to maintain a beginner's mind-set, but I have to admit it's often difficult. To help me do it, I try to always keep the following three things in mind:

1. Everyone has something to teach me.
2. Every day I have something to learn.
3. Every time I learn something, I benefit.

The other thing I do is focus on asking questions. For too many years I concentrated on giving answers. As a young leader, I felt that was expected of me. But as soon as I started to get over my insecurity, I discovered that asking questions did more for my development than answering them, and the moment I intentionally asked questions and started listening, my personal and professional growth took off. Asking questions can do the same for you.

3. Teachable People Take Long, Hard Looks in the Mirror

Novelist James Thom remarked, "Probably the most honest, 'self-made' man ever was the one we heard say: 'I got to the top the hard way—fighting my own laziness and ignorance every step of the way.'" Can you relate to that statement? I certainly can. I'm known for writing and speaking on leadership, but the most difficult person I have ever led is me!

Becoming and remaining teachable requires people to honestly and openly evaluate themselves on a continual basis. Any time you face a challenge, loss, or problem, one of the first things you need to ask yourself is, "Am I the cause?" This is a key to teachability. If the answer is yes, then you need to be ready to make changes. Otherwise you're going to experience what one wit called "déjà-poo," the feeling you've been in this mess before.

When people refuse to look in the mirror and instead look to other people or situations to blame, they keep getting the same result over and over. Recognizing your own part in your failings, seeking solutions (no matter how painful), and working hard to put them into place is teachability in action. And it leads to the ability to change, grow, and move forward in life.

Physician William Mayo prayed, "Lord, deliver me from the man who never makes a mistake, and also from the man who makes the same mistake twice." There's nothing wrong with making mistakes, but some people respond with encores. A teachable spirit will help to put a stop to that.

4. Teachable People Encourage Others to Speak into Their Lives

Teachable people need to surround themselves with people who know them well and who will lovingly, yet honestly, speak into their life. However, that can be a challenge—for many reasons. First, you must be willing to develop strong enough relationships with people that you can credibly ask them to speak into your life. Second, they must be courageous and honest enough to speak freely to you. And third, you must be willing to accept their feedback and criticism without defending yourself. Otherwise, you'll receive it only once!

That process becomes further complicated if you are highly successful. When you are influential and highly respected, people tend to tell you what you want to hear, not what you *need* to hear. They are seeking your approval, or they flatter you. Unfortunately, that creates a gap between what you hear and reality. If you find yourself in that situation, you will need to work extra hard to get the people close to you to speak honesty into your life. And you will have to become highly intentional in observing and listening.

Everybody needs someone who is willing to speak into his life. Ideally, it should be someone who is above you organizationally or ahead of you experientially. Look for clues that you may be off track, and ask people to verify your suspicions. They will be more likely to speak freely if you've brought up your deficiency first.

5. Teachable People Learn Something New Every Day

The secret to any person's success can be found in his or her daily agenda. People grow and improve not by huge leaps and bounds but by small, incremental changes. Children's advocate Marian Wright Edelman said, "We must not, in trying to think about how we can make a big difference, ignore the small daily differences we can make which, over time, add up to big differences that we often cannot foresee." She understands that progress comes day by day, inch by inch.

Teachable people try to leverage this truth by learning something new every day. A single day is enough to make us a little larger or a little smaller. Several single days strung together will make us a lot larger or a lot smaller. If we do that every day, day upon day, there is great power for change.

The habits you practice every day will make you or break you. If you want to become a teachable person who learns from losses, then make learning your daily habit. It may not change your life in a day. But it will change your days for life.

Daily Practices to Become More Teachable

If you believe in the idea of trying to learn something new every day, but you don't know the best way to go about it, then I recommend that you engage in the following three practices every day.

1. Preparation

If you want to be ready to meet whatever challenges you're going to face on a given day and learn from them, you need to be prepared. That means working in advance—every day. As my old mentor John Wooden used to say, "When opportunity comes, it's too late to prepare."

How do I go about preparing for my day so that I can learn from it? I start each morning by looking at my schedule. As I review my commitments for the day, I ask myself some questions:

- Where are the potential learning moments for today?
- Who will I meet and what can I ask them?
- What will I experience and what might I be able to learn from it?

By looking for the probable teaching moments and preparing for them, I make learning possible.

You don't have to spend hours in preparation every day, though you may sometimes have things on your schedule that would warrant such preparation. Just plan to spend a few minutes each morning or the evening before thinking through what your day will be like and where the greatest potential opportunities lie for you to learn. You will be amazed by how often you can improve yourself just drawing on the people and experiences that are part of your daily life.

2. Contemplation

Time alone is essential to learning. Contemplation allows people to observe and reflect on the occurrences of their lives and derive meaning from them. Stopping and thinking allows us to gain perspective on both the successes and failures of our day so that we can find the lessons within them. It also enables you to plan how you can improve in the future.

It's good to remember that there's much to learn from negative experiences. In science, mistakes always precede discoveries. It is impossible to make discoveries without an accumulation of errors. To a scientist, a mistake is not failure—it's feedback. Using that feedback, a scientist can ask not just "What happened?" but also "What does it mean?" That comes from using critical thinking skills. Without them, we miss the meaning of the occurrences in our lives.

When the lessons we learn come from mistakes, we must first determine if the mistake was due to ignorance or stupidity. *Ignorance* means we didn't have the necessary information; *stupidity* means we had the necessary information but misused it.

As you spend time in contemplation, ask yourself questions like these:

- What can I learn from what I read today?
- What can I learn from what I saw today?
- What can I learn from what I heard today?
- What can I learn from what I experienced today?
- What can I learn from what I did wrong today?
- What can I learn from whom I met today?
- What can I learn from what I discussed today?

I recommend that you set aside thirty minutes at the end of every day to think about the preceding twenty-four hours, contemplating what occurred and what you can learn from it. Not only will that help you to remain teachable, but you will also learn something every day because of the process.

3. Application

The true value of teachability comes when we take something that we learn and apply it. We can learn a lot from our mistakes if we remain teachable. Not everyone does that. When people make mistakes, they generally do one of three things in response to them: They resolve to never make another mistake, which is impossible. They allow their mistakes to make them into cowards, which is foolish. In contrast, successful people make up their minds to learn from their mistakes and apply the lessons to their lives, which is profitable. That's how they win.

I try to learn something new every day. And because I do that, the pool of what I'm learning keeps growing, not diminishing. A friend recently asked me how many more books I want to write. I don't have a specific number. The answer will be determined by whether I remain teachable and keep applying what I discover. As long as I'm still learning, I will continue to have something to say.

8

Overcome Adversity
The Catalyst for Learning

I believe that one of the times people change is when they hurt enough that they have to. Writer and professor Robertson Davies said, "Extraordinary people survive under the most terrible circumstances and then become more extraordinary because of it." The pain of adversity never leaves us the same, yet treated right, it can be the catalyst for positive change.

Most of the time we don't choose our adversity, but all the time we can choose our response to it. *If* we respond positively to difficulties, the outcome will be potentially positive. *If* we respond negatively to our difficulties, the outcome will be potentially negative. That's why I call our response "the *if* factor."

There's a story about a young woman who complained to her father about her life and how hard things were for her. The adversity of life was overwhelming her, and she wanted to give up.

As he listened, her father filled three pots with water and brought them to a boil on the stove. Into the first he put carrot slices, into the second he put eggs, and into the third he put ground coffee beans. He let them simmer for a few minutes and then placed the carrots, eggs, and coffee before her in three containers.

"What do you see?" he asked.

"Carrots, eggs, and coffee," she replied.

He asked her to feel the carrots. She picked up a piece and it squished between her fingers. He then asked her to examine an egg. She picked one up, broke the shell, and saw the hard-boiled egg inside it. Finally, he asked her to sip the coffee. She smiled as she tasted its rich flavor.

"So what does it mean?" she asked.

"Each ingredient was subjected to the same thing—boiling water—but each reacted differently. The carrots went in hard. But after they were in the boiling water, they became soft. The egg was fragile with a thin outer shell and a liquid interior. But it became hardened. The ground coffee beans changed little. But they changed the water for the better.

"Which are you," he asked. "When you face adversity, how do you respond? Are you a carrot, an egg, or a coffee bean?"

Life is filled with adversity. We can be squashed by it.

We can allow it to make us hard. Or we can make the best of it, improving the situation. As British prime minister Winston Churchill noted, "I have derived continued benefit from criticism at all periods of my life, and I do not remember any time when I was ever short of it." Since you will face adversity, why not make the best of it?

The Advantages of Adversity

Adversity is a catalyst for learning. It can actually create advantages for you *if* you face it with the right mind-set. It all depends on how you respond to it. Here's what I mean:

1. Adversity Introduces Us to Ourselves If We Want to Know Ourselves

Adversity always gets our attention. We can't ignore it. It causes us to stop and look at our situation. And at ourselves if we have the courage. Adversity is an opportunity for self-discovery. As the great Egyptian leader Anwar el-Sadat said, "Great suffering builds up a human being and puts him within the reach of self-knowledge." This I believe is true—if we embrace it that way.

Unfortunately, many people choose to hide during times of adversity. They build walls, close their eyes, run away, medicate themselves, or do whatever they must to avoid dealing with the reality of the situation. They are like Sergeant Schulz in the old TV comedy *Hogan's Heroes*. Anytime something happens that they don't want to acknowledge, they say, "I know nothing. I see nothing." If that is your response to adversity, you will never understand the situation or yourself.

One of my favorite books is *As a Man Thinketh* by James Allen. My father required me to read it when I was in junior high school. One of the ideas that left the strongest impression on me as a youth was this: "Circumstance does not make the man; it reveals him to himself." That is true, but only *if* you allow it to.

Adversity has introduced me to myself in many times during my lifetime. It has opened my eyes. It has plumbed the depths of my heart. It has tested my strength. And it has taught me a lot. Here are a few of the lessons I've learned:

• When I have gotten off track and am seemingly lost, I have learned that the road to success is not always a road.

• When I have been exhausted and frustrated, I have learned that trying times are not the time to stop trying.

• When I have been discouraged with my progress, I have learned not to let what I was doing get to me before I got to it.

• When I have failed, I have learned that I will not be judged by the number of times I have failed but by the number of times I succeed.

Adversity has introduced me to tenacity, creativity, focus, and many other positive things that have helped me to like myself better. Novelist and songwriter Samuel Lover asserted, "Circumstances are the rulers of the weak; but they are the instruments of the wise." If I respond negatively to my circumstances, they will keep me enslaved to them. If I respond wisely, my circumstances will serve me.

2. Adversity Is a Better Teacher Than Success If We Want to Learn from Adversity

Adversity comes to us as a teaching tool. You've probably heard the saying, "When the pupil is ready the teacher will come." That is not necessarily true. With adversity, the teacher will come whether the pupil is ready or not. Those who are ready learn from the teacher. Those who are not don't learn.

Philosopher and author Emmet Fox said, "It is the Law that many difficulties that can come to you at any time, no matter what they are, must be exactly what you need at the moment, to enable you to take the next step forward by overcoming them. The only real misfortune, the only real tragedy comes when we suffer without learning the lesson." The key to avoiding that tragedy is *wanting* to learn from life's difficulties.

Oprah Winfrey's advice to "turn your wounds into wisdom" can come true for us only *if* we want to learn from our wounds. It requires the right mind-set and a deliberate intention to find the lesson in the loss. If we don't embrace those things, then all we end up with is the scars.

3. Adversity Opens Doors for New Opportunities
If We Want to Learn from It

One of the greatest lessons I've learned as a leader is that adversity is often the door to opportunity. Successful entrepreneurs know this instinctively, but most people have been trained to see adversity the wrong way. As speaker and cofounder of the Rich Dad Company, Kim Kiyosaki, observed, "Most of us are taught, beginning in kindergarten, that mistakes are bad. How often did you hear, 'Don't make a mistake!' In reality, the way we learn is by *making* mistakes. A mistake simply shows you something you didn't know. Once you make the mistake, then you know it. Think about the first time you touched a hot stove (the mistake). From making that mistake, you learned that if you touch a hot stove you get burned. A mistake isn't bad; it's there to teach you something."

When many people face adversity, they let it get them down. Instead, they need to look for the benefit or opportunity. Any time you face difficulties, are you seeing the opportunities? Are you looking for ways to take advantage of them? When real estate prices are down, there is an opportunity. Do you see it? When interest rates are down, that brings opportunities. Business needs are changing; that provides a wealth of opportunities. Every adversity brings an advantage. Are you trying to make the most of it? Or are you letting adversity get you down?

4. Adversity Can Signal a Coming Positive Transition If We Respond Correctly to It

In 1915, the people of Coffee City, Alabama, were devastated after their cotton crop was destroyed by boll weevils. The area's entire economy was built on cotton. What would they do? Scientist George Washington Carver suggested that local farmers grow peanuts.

When the crop came in, Carver was able to show how peanuts could be used to create chemicals needed to make soap, ink, plastics, and cosmetics. It opened up the economy to new crops, new ideas, and a brighter future. Today peanuts are still a vital crop in the southern United States. How fortunate it was for everyone that Carver has seen the opportunity for a transition that adversity had provided.

The life of a successful person is comprised of one transition after another. Being static isn't an option in life. Time is always moving forward. We can't stop it, nor can we stop its effects. We need to make changes, and adversity can often be the catalyst. James Allen wrote, "Let a person rejoice when he is confronted with obstacles, for it means that he has reached the end of some particular line of indifference or folly, and is now called upon to summon up all his energy and intelligence in order to extricate himself, and to find a better way; that the powers within him are crying out for greater freedom, for enlarged exercise and scope."

5. Adversity Brings Profit as Well as Pain
If We Expect It and Plan for It

In life we should all expect pain. It's a part of life. It's a part of loss. The question is, are you going to let it stop you from doing what you want and need to do? Or are you going to learn from it and use the experience to help you win?

No one ever says, "Go for the silver." Athletes, coaches, and fans always say, "Go for the gold!" Why? Because gold represents the best. If you're going to endure the pain it takes to compete, why not compete to win?

Successful people expect to experience pain when they face adversity. They plan for it. And by planning for it, they set themselves up to benefit from it. Fred Smith once said, "I listened to Bob Richards, the Olympic gold medalist, interview younger Olympian winners of the gold. He asked them, 'What did you do when you began to hurt?'" Fred points out that none of the Olympians was surprised by the question. They expected pain, and they had a strategy for dealing with it. As Bob Richards summed up, "You never win the gold without hurting."

6. Adversity Writes Our Story, and If Our Response
Is Right, the Story Will Be Good

Some people treat adversity as a stepping-stone, others as a tombstone. The difference in the way they approach it depends on how they see it. Performance psychologist

Jim Loehr says, "Champions have taught us how to take an experience and essentially write the story of its effect. If you see a failure as an opportunity to learn and get better, it will be. If you perceive it as a mortal blow, it will be. In that way, the power of the story is more important than the experience itself."

When you respond right to adversity, you see it as something that can help you to become better than you were before. What kind of story will adversity write in your life? I hope yours will be positive.

Adversity without triumph is not inspiring; it's depressing. Adversity without growth is not encouraging; it's discouraging. The great potential story in adversity is one of hope and success. Adversity is everyone's, but the story you write with your life is yours alone. Everyone gets a chance to be the hero in a potentially great story. Some step up to that role and some don't. The choice is yours.

9

Expect Problems

Opportunities for Learning

I think it's important to remember that everyone has problems, no matter how high or low their station in life. We sometimes look at the lives of others, and if they are highly successful and seem to have it all together, we assume that they don't have problems. Or we believe their problems are easier to deal with than ours. That's a false belief. For example, Jeff Immelt is the CEO of General Electric, a position most leaders would greatly respect. People might think Immelt's lofty position would protect him from problems. But Immelt said this after the September 11 attack: "My second day as chairman, a plane that I lease, flying with engines I built, crashed into a building that I insure, and it was covered with a network I own." That's a day with a lot of problems.

Don't Do This...

The key to overcoming problems and learning from them is to approach them the right way. Over the years, I've learned that problems get better or worse based on what you do or don't do when you face them. First, let me give you the don'ts:

1. Don't Underestimate the Problem

Many problems go unresolved or are managed ineffectively because we do not take them seriously enough. Years ago I read a wonderful book by Robert H. Schuller titled *Tough Times Never Last, But Tough People Do!* The following paragraph helped me as a young leader to find a more realistic view of my problems and myself:

> Never underestimate a problem or your power to cope with it. Realize that the problem you are facing has been faced by millions of human beings. You have untapped potential for dealing with a problem if you will take the problem and your own undeveloped, unchanneled powers seriously. Your reaction to a problem, as much as the problem itself, will determine the outcome. I have seen people face the most catastrophic problems with a positive mental attitude, turning their problems into creative experiences. They turned their scars into stars.[6]

When I first read that paragraph, I became inspired. It made me believe that the size of the person is more important than the size of the problem.

2. Don't Overestimate the Problem

Some people experience one problem three or more times. They experience it the first time when they worry about the problem. They experience it the second time when it actually occurs. And they live it again as they keep reliving it!

I've done that. Have you? When faced with a problem, my first instinct is often to exaggerate its impact. Do that and you may be defeated before the problem ever occurs!

In an interview, leadership author and professor John Kotter said that one of his executive students gave him a two-page letter that his CEO had sent out. Part One said, "We're in a mess. Denial doesn't help. Here are some statistics to show it."

Part Two said, "It is useful to look at history. Thirty years ago this company was in a worse mess. Look at us now. We're ten times bigger. The U.S. economy had deeper recessions every twenty years in the nineteenth century. And here we are—the most powerful nation on earth."

Part Three said, "We've got to link arms and address this thing, and it's going to start with me. I'm going to try my damnedest to figure out (1) how this doesn't hurt us and (2) how we can find opportunities in this. Because there are opportunities."

The last part was, "Here's what I'm going to do, and here's what I need your help with." The final note was hopeful but not naïve.

It seems to me that the CEO was doing his best to neither underestimate nor overestimate the problem the company was facing, but rather to look at it realistically and tackle it.

3. Don't Wait for the Problem to Solve Itself

That brings us to the next lesson I've learned about problems. You can't wait for them to solve themselves. Patience is a virtue in problem solving if you are at the same time doing all that you can to fix the situation. It is not a virtue if you are waiting, hoping that the problem will solve itself or just go away.

Problems demand that we pay them attention. Why? Because left alone they almost always get worse. Nina DiSesa, who led the ad agency McCann Erickson in the late 1990s, observed, "When you step into a turnaround situation, you can safely assume four things: morale is low, fear is high, the good people are halfway out the door, and the slackers are hiding." Those things won't improve on their own. They require intentional problem solving and active leadership.

4. Don't Aggravate the Problem

Not only do problems not solve themselves, but we can actually make them worse by how we respond to them. One of the things I've told staff members for years is that problems are like fires, and every person carries around two buckets. One bucket has water, and the other gasoline. When you come across a problem, you can use the bucket of water to try to put the fire out. Or you can pour gasoline on it and make it explode. Same problem, two different results.

Taking a potentially volatile situation and making it worse is only one way of aggravating a problem. We can also make problems worse when we respond to them poorly. Some of the ways we can do that include:

- Losing our perspective
- Giving up important priorities and values
- Losing our sense of humor
- Feeling sorry for ourselves
- Blaming others for our situation

Instead, we need to try to remain positive. Author Norman Vincent Peale asserted, "Positive thinking is how you think about a problem. Enthusiasm is how you feel about a problem. The two together determine what you do about a problem."

Do This...

If you want to overcome problems and turn them into opportunities for learning, then I recommend that you do the following:

1. Do Anticipate the Problem

They say the punch that knocks you out is not necessarily the hardest one, but the one you didn't see coming. I once read about a prisoner in Sydney, Australia, who succeeded in breaking out of jail. He hid in the underpinnings of a delivery truck that had stopped briefly in the prison warehouse. He held on desperately as the truck drove out of the prison. A few moments later, when the truck finally stopped, the prisoner dropped down to the ground and rolled outward to freedom. Unfortunately he discovered that he was now in the courtyard of another prison five miles from the first. He sure didn't see that coming.

Of course, anticipating problems doesn't mean worrying all the time about everything that *could* go wrong. I enjoy the story of a man who was awakened by his wife. She thought she heard a burglar downstairs. He slowly got up, went grumpily downstairs, and found himself staring into the barrel of a gun. The burglar ordered him to hand over all the household valuables, then started to leave. The husband stopped him. "Before you go," he said, "I'd like you to come upstairs and meet my wife. She's been expecting you every night for over thirty years."

2. Do Communicate the Problem

Former college football head coach Lou Holtz quipped, "Don't tell your problems to people! Eighty percent don't care and the other 20 percent are glad you have them." I laugh every time I think about that statement, because for the most part it is true. On the other hand, if we work with other people, we *must* communicate about our problem to the people whom it will affect. We owe them that. Besides the solution often lies in receiving help from someone else who is able to help us solve it.

Whenever I'm preparing to communicate regarding a problem, I first try to gather information and find out people's experiences and perspectives. That process helps me to understand better what's going on and where everyone is coming from. Sometimes I find out that the problem we have isn't the problem I thought it was. Occasionally, I discover that the problem I was concerned about wasn't actually a problem at all. Or that people on the team are already solving it. But no matter what, whether it involves family, friends, employees, or teammates, when you are facing problems, it's crucial that you all get on the same page and work on it together.

3. Do Evaluate the Problem

They say you should never open a can of worms unless you plan to go fishing. Too often, I've been quick to open up the can without first thinking through the situation. I would have been better off trying to evaluate first.

How do you do that? First, you need to ask yourself, *What is the issue?* If someone says the moon is a hundred miles from Earth, no big deal. Let it go. Unless you're a scientist, it doesn't matter. If someone is about to eat food that is poisoned, deal with it immediately. You have to adjust to the size and weight of the issue. Sometimes that's hard to do, especially for a type A person who wants to jump in on every little thing. To keep myself from doing that, for years I had a laminated card on my desk with the question, "Does this REALLY MATTER?" It helped me keep perspective when an issue was being discussed.

The second question you need to ask is, *Who is involved?* Often problems are problems because of the people in the middle of them. Some are like Charlie Brown in the classic *Peanuts* television special *A Charlie Brown Christmas*. When he just can't seem to get into the Christmas spirit, Linus tells him, "You're the only person I know who can take a wonderful season like Christmas and turn it into a problem."

As you evaluate problems, try to maintain perspective, and always keep the end in mind. I saw something when I lived in southern Indiana that captures this idea concisely. It was a sign on a farm fence that said, "If you cross this field you had better do it in 9.8 seconds. The bull can do it in 10 seconds."

4. Do Appreciate the Problem

Appreciating a problem is counterintuitive for many people. Most people see a problem as a nuisance and try to avoid it. However, if we have the right attitude and appreciate a problem, not only will we work harder to solve it, but we will also learn and grow from it. Problems always bring opportunities, and opportunities always bring problems. The two go hand in hand. If we can learn to appreciate that truth, we have a real advantage in life.

A problem isn't really a problem unless you allow it to be a problem. A problem is really an opportunity. If you can see it that way, then every time you face a problem, you will realize that you're really faced with an opportunity. At the least, it's an opportunity to learn. But it could become even more if you pursue solving it with the right attitude.

If you want to gain the full benefit from every problem, challenge, and loss, stop looking for the back door and face the difficulty with the determination to gain something from it. Do that, and you can become a hero in your own life.

10

Understand Bad Experiences

The Perspective for Learning

Back in the year 2000, I was working on my book *The 17 Indisputable Laws of Teamwork*. About a month before the manuscript was due, I was scheduled to go on a two-week speaking tour in Africa. *What a great opportunity to finish writing the book*, I thought. And it was. I can still remember the satisfaction I felt at Victoria Falls, when I finished the work. It was on the very day I was to return to the United States. With a great sense of completion and fulfillment, I put the manuscript into my briefcase and headed home.

When I arrived back in the United States, my son-in-law Steve picked me up at the Atlanta airport. After the long flight, I was hungry, so we stopped to pick up some Mexican food on our way out of Atlanta, and off we went.

As Steve drove, I rode in the passenger seat and got ready to eat, but I managed to drop my fork. I tried to reach down and find it, but it was hopeless. "Steve, pull over, will you?" I finally asked. And Steve, who is used to this sort of thing from me, pulled over to the side of the road so that I could make my search. I got out, moved my briefcase, which was sitting beside me on the floor, and there was the fork. Fantastic! I could finally eat! I climbed back in, and off we went. About twenty minutes later, after I'd finished my food, I looked over and said, "Where's my briefcase?" That's when it hit me. When I was looking for the fork, I had taken out my briefcase and set it on the side of the road. *And I never put it back in the car!*

The loss of the briefcase would be bad enough, but you have to understand that when I write, I don't use a computer. I write everything out on a legal pad by hand. There is no backup. There's only one copy, and that copy represents months of work. That one copy of the manuscript was in my briefcase.

We had gone twenty miles by the time I realized what I had done. The instant I figured it out, we turned around and went back to the place we had stopped. But the briefcase and my manuscript were gone!

Over the next several days, I was overwhelmed with emotions. I felt:

• *Stupidity:* I wondered how anyone could be smart enough to write a book and dumb enough to leave it on the side of the road.

- *Anxiety:* It was hopeless to think I'd ever see my brief-case again, so I spent hours writing down whatever I could remember from the manuscript. After a couple of days, I came to the conclusion that I could rewrite the book, but it would take at least six months. And because I was feeling so low emotionally, I felt certain that it would not be as good as the original.

- *Frustration:* It looked like there was no way to meet my publisher's deadline. I had wasted months of my time. If only I had made a copy. But I hadn't.

- *Despair:* Then I started to doubt myself. *What if I couldn't rewrite the book at all?* I wondered.

While I was feeling discouraged, my assistant Linda Eggers was undaunted. She started calling local police precincts to see if the briefcase had been turned in to them. On the fourth day, Linda struck gold. The briefcase had been turned in. Better yet, everything was still in it—including the manuscript. We all rejoiced, the book was published, and all was well. However, even to this day, whenever I pick up *The 17 Indisputable Laws of Teamwork*, I think of my bad experience and the lessons I learned from it, which includes always giving Linda each chapter of a manuscript as I finish it.

Putting Your Losses into Perspective

Obviously, no one goes out of the way to have bad experiences. But the truth is that the negative experiences we have can do us some good, if we are willing to let them. The next time you have a bad experience, allow it to help you do the following:

1. Accept Your Humanness

No matter how hard we try, no matter how talented we are, no matter how high our standards may be, we will fail. Why? Because we're human. Nobody is perfect, and when we have bad experiences, we should allow that to be a reminder to us that we need to accept our imperfections.

When you have a bad experience, I hope you will give yourself some grace—whether it's a matter beyond your control or because you made a mistake. You're only human, and you shouldn't expect yourself to be perfect.

2. Learn to Laugh at Yourself and Life

I have discovered that if I'm willing to see the humor in my bad experiences, I will never run out of things to laugh about. Does laughing fix everything? Maybe not. But it does help us. Laughter is like changing a baby's diaper—it doesn't permanently solve any problems, but it makes things more acceptable for a while.

Sometimes it's hard to see the humor during a difficult experience. Often I say to myself, "This is not funny today, but tomorrow it may be." How much lighter would your load be if you were to find ways to laugh when you were faced with bad experiences?

3. Keep the Right Perspective

When you have a bad experience, which of the following phrases is most likely to represent your thinking?

- I never wanted to do that task to start with, so who cares?
- I'm a failure and my life is over.
- I want to give up and never try again.
- I'm gaining experience from my mistakes; I wonder if I can get some help.
- I now know three ways that won't work, so I'll try again.

Your answer says more about your perspective than it does about the bad experience. That's why the responses to the same bad experience can be so varied.

Author and speaker Denis Waitley says, "Mistakes are painful when they happen, but years later a collection of mistakes is what is called experience." Seeing difficulties as experience is a matter of perspective. It's like the difference between going in the ocean as a small child and as an adult. When you're little, the waves look massive, and you fear that they may overwhelm you. As an adult, the same size waves may be seen as a source of relaxation and fun.

When facing difficulties, maintaining perspective isn't always easy, but it is worth fighting for. As you work to maintain the right point of view, try to keep these three things in mind.

DON'T BASE YOUR SELF-WORTH ON A BAD EXPERIENCE

You are not your performance. And you don't have to be defined by your worst moments. So don't base your self-image on those things. Instead, try to understand and accept your value as a human being. If you fail, don't ever tell yourself, "I am a failure." Instead, keep things in perspective and say, "I may have missed that one, but I'm still okay. I can still be a winner!"

DON'T FEEL SORRY FOR YOURSELF

One of the worst things you can do to lose perspective is to start feeling sorry for yourself. Okay, if you have a bad experience, you can feel sorry for yourself for twenty-four hours, but then after that, pick yourself up and get moving again. Because if you start to wallow, you just might get stuck. If you find yourself in the aftermath of a bad experience, try to remember that if you're still breathing, it could have been worse. Try to focus on the good you can make of the difficulty. Because of the experience you've gained, you may even be able to help others who have gone through similar difficulties.

DO CONSIDER YOUR FAILURES AS A PROCESS TO LEARN AND IMPROVE

When we fail or have a bad experience, we need to learn to become more like scientists and inventors. When their work fails, they call it an experiment that didn't work. Or they say they tested a hypothesis. Or they term it data collection. They keep their perspective, avoid taking it personally, learn from it, and leverage it for future success. What a great way to look at things.

4. Don't Give Up

Swimmer Eric Shanteau has called the 2004 U.S. Olympic Swim Trials "the most devastating experience of my life." That's quite a statement considering Shanteau was diagnosed with cancer in 2008. What would make those Olympic trails such a difficult experience? He finished third—and only the first two places in the trials make the Olympic team. In fact, it happened twice during those trials. He missed second place in the 400-meter individual medley by 0.99 seconds and the 200-meter individual medley by 0.34 seconds.

He may have wanted to give up, but he didn't. He got back in the pool and trained for another four years. His reward in 2008 was making the team in the 200-meter breaststroke. Though he didn't medal in Beijing, he did swim a personal best. He kept training and returned to the Olympics again in 2012 in London. He won a gold medal by swimming the breaststroke for the team in the 4×100-meter medley relay.

What does Shanteau know about bad experiences that most people don't? He knows that:

- Failure is the cost of seeking new challenges.
- Ninety percent of those who fail are not actually defeated; they simply quit.
- There are two kinds of people in regards to setbacks: splatters, who hit the bottom, fall apart, and stay on the bottom; and bouncers, who hit rock bottom, pull themselves together, and bounce back up.
- Success lies in having made the effort; failure lies in never having tried.
- Most failures are people who have the habit of making excuses.

If you want to succeed in life, you can't give up.

5. Don't Let Your Bad Experience Become a Worse Experience

One of the things that's worse than a bad experience is letting that bad experience become an even worse one—if you have the power to stop it. How do you gain the power to recognize when an experience is going from bad to worse? By learning from previous experiences using critical thinking skills.

If you find yourself in a bad experience, one of the first things you should try to do is determine if the bad experience is a result of ignorance or stupidity. Ignorance means that you didn't have the necessary knowledge to do the right thing. A person can hardly be blamed for that. Stupidity is the result of knowing what to do but not acting upon that knowledge. Bad experiences based on ignorance require learning. If you have a teachable spirit, as I discussed in chapter seven, not only can you stop a bad experience from getting worse, you can make it better. On the other hand, bad experiences based on stupidity usually come from lack of discipline and poor choices. Changing those requires not only teachability but also a change in behavior. If you don't make those changes, the bad experiences will likely keep coming and keep getting worse.

6. Let the Bad Experience Lead You to a Good Experience

Everyone can relate to having bad experiences in life. But not everyone works to turn the bad experiences into good ones. That is possible only when we turn our losses into learning experiences. You just have to remember that bad experiences are bad only if we fail to learn from them. And good experiences are almost always a result of previous bad experiences.

For years I have been a pen collector. Maybe that's because I actually use a pen, not a computer, when I write. In my search for interesting pens, I came across an intriguing story about a young insurance agent who had been working to win a new client for quite a long time. Finally, he was successful and persuaded the man to take out a large policy.

The agent arrived at the potential client's office with the contract ready for a signature. He placed it on the man's desk and took out a fountain pen. But as he removed the pen's cap, it leaked ink all over the contract, ruining it.

The agent prepared another contract as quickly as he could, but by the time he returned, the window of opportunity was closed. The would-be client had changed his mind and declined to give the agent his business.

The young agent was so disgusted with the pen and the problem it had caused that he devoted his time to the development of a reliable fountain pen. That young agent was Lewis E. Waterman, and his company has been in the business of producing fine pens for 120 years. He not only took a bad experience and turned it into a good experience, but he created a well-respected and lucrative business from it. That's really turning a setback into a step forward.

11

Embrace Change

The Price of Learning

Change is difficult for all of us, yet it is essential if we want to turn our losses into gains. It is the price we must pay for learning. And don't let anyone tell you, "You can't teach an old dog new tricks." A lot of dog trainers have proven that statement to be false. Besides, the ideas in this chapter are not written for old dogs and they are not about tricks. They are for people like you and me who want to change, learn, and grow. We can do these things—if we're willing to pay the price.

Why People Resist Change

Change is not embraced by most people. I used to think leaders loved change and everyone else didn't. Now after decades of teaching and investing in leaders, I have come to realize that leaders resist change as much as followers

do—unless the change is their idea! The truth is that just
about everybody resists change. Why? Because...

Change Can Feel Like a Personal Loss

Novelist Andre Gide observed, "One doesn't discover new
lands without consenting to lose sight of the shore for a
very long time." That loss can be very frightening, and it
can sometimes feel like a personal loss. But the truth of
the matter is that though change *feels* personal, it isn't. The
world keeps changing and it affects everyone, whether they
like it or not.

Poet and philosopher Ralph Waldo Emerson had an
insightful take on this. He asserted, "For every thing we
gain we lose something." We like gaining, but we don't like
losing. We want to have the one without the other. But life
doesn't work that way. Every beginning ends something.
Every ending begins something new. We are continually
making trades in life. Unfortunately, if you resist change,
you are trading your potential to grow for your comfort. No
change means no growth.

Change Feels Awkward

Change always feels different. Because it's unfamiliar, it
often doesn't feel right. Let me give you an example. Take a
moment right now and clasp your hands together with your
fingers interlaced. That probably feels very comfortable.
Why? Because you naturally place your hands a certain

way, with one thumb over the other. Now clasp your hands the opposite way by trading the position of your thumbs and moving your fingers one place over from where you usually interlock them. How does that feel? It's probably uncomfortable. Why? You never clasp your hands that way.

Is it wrong to clasp your hands this other way? No. Is it an inferior way of clasping hands? No. It's just different. And different feels awkward. But you *can* get used to it. Don't believe me? Every day for the next two weeks, clasp your hands the opposite way from what you're used to. By the end of that time, it will feel almost as comfortable as your natural way.

Change Goes Against Tradition

When I received my first leadership position in an organization, I can't tell you how many times I heard the phrase "We've never done it that way before." It seemed like every time I wanted to make an improvement, I heard someone extol the virtues of resisting change. I can't tell you how frustrating that was, especially when the person who said it couldn't tell me *why* it had always been done the way it had been done. There's nothing wrong with tradition, as long as a person doesn't become a slave to it. The person who insists on using yesterday's methods in today's world won't be in business tomorrow.

Some people believe that nothing should ever be done until everyone is convinced that it ought to be done. The problem with that is it takes so long to convince them that by the time they finally agree to the change, it's time to move on to something else. No wonder some people believe that progress means moving backward slowly.

How People Respond to Change

Because people don't like change, most of them don't react to it very well. And their response creates more problems for them. Here's what I mean:

Most People Change Only Enough to Get Away from Problems, Not Enough to Fix Them

Most people would rather change their circumstances to improve their lives when instead they need to change themselves to improve their circumstances. They put in just enough effort to distance themselves from their problems without ever trying to go after the root, which can often be found in themselves. Because they don't try to change the source of their problems, their problems keep coming back at them. Positive change and a willingness to learn are personal responsibilities. If you want to get better, you need to be willing to change.

Most People Do the Same Thing the Same Way, Yet Expect Different Results

Whenever we try something and it fails, why do we keep trying the exact same thing expecting to get different results? It doesn't make sense. What do we expect to change? Our luck? The laws of physics? How can our lives get better if we don't change? How can we become better if we don't expose ourselves to growing situations and people?

Our lives are like a trip we plan to a distant city. We set a destination, map out our route, and start driving. But we should know there will be detours and obstacles ahead. Do we ignore those and pretend they don't exist? How successful will we be if we think, *The obstacles and conditions need to adjust to me because I'm not changing*? Not very. We need to be willing to make adjustments. Tenacity is a fantastic quality. But tenacity without a willingness to change and make necessary adjustments becomes dogmatism and leads to dead ends.

Most People See Change as a Hurtful Necessity Instead of a Helpful Opportunity

Let's face the fact: change is messy. But life is change. Being born was painful. Learning to eat was messy. Learning to walk was difficult and painful. In fact, most of the things you needed to learn in order to live were tough on you. But when you were a small child, you didn't know any better, and you did what you needed to do to learn and grow. Now that you're an adult, you have a choice. Do you want to avoid the potential pain or endure it and pursue the opportunity?

Every time you embrace change, there is an opportunity for you to go in a positive direction, make improvements to yourself, and abandon old negative habits and ways of thinking. Change allows you to examine your assumptions, rethink your strategies, and build your relationships. Without change there is no innovation, creativity, or improvement. If you are willing and able to initiate change, you will have a better opportunity to manage the change that is inevitable to everyone in life.

Most People Won't Pay the Immediate Price to Change and End Up Paying the Ultimate Price for Not Changing

Change always requires something of us. We must pay a price for it. In fact, ongoing change and improvement require continual payment. But the process begins with the *first* payment. That first payment starts the growth process. If that first price remains unpaid, there is no growth or learning. And what will that cost you in the end? You lose potential and gain regret.

As I grow older, I have come to realize that most of our regrets will not be a result of what we did. They will come because of what we could and should have done but didn't do. The final price we pay is called missed opportunity, and that is a heavy cost.

Most People Change Only When Prompted by One of Three Things

In the end, because people are so resistant to it, change occurs only under certain conditions. In my experience, people change when:

- They *hurt* enough that they *have* to.
- They *learn* enough that they *want* to.
- They *receive* enough that they are *able* to.

Unless one of those things happens, people don't want to change. Sometimes people require all three to happen before they are willing to change.

Making the Changes That Count

If you want to maximize your ability to pay the price of learning and set yourself up to change, improve, and grow, then you need to do the five following things:

1. Change Yourself

Back when I used to do a lot of marriage counseling for couples, I found that most people came into the process intent on seeing the other person change. I believe that is part of the human condition: to look for the faults in others and minimize our own. But that's not how you improve any relationship. If you want to see positive change in your marriage, quit looking for a better person and become a better person. If you want to see positive change in your career, quit looking for a better employer and become a better employee. In life, if you want more, you must become more. And if changing yourself seems overwhelming, then start with something small.

2. Change Your Attitude

Trying to change others is an exercise in futility. No one can change another person. I didn't always know this. For many years my life was filled with disappointments over other people's unwillingness to grow. Anything you try to change that is outside of your control will ultimately disappoint you. What's worse, I have also discovered that when I try to change those things that are outside of my control, I start to lose control of those things within me that I can change because my focus is wrong. That's a trap to be avoided.

What's the solution? Changing my attitude. That is completely within my control, and the beauty of it is that this one change can be a major factor in changing my life for the positive. In controlling my own attitude and choosing to think correctly, I can minimize the negative effects of those around me who have bad attitudes. I can stop taking it personally when someone in my life won't change. I can see opportunities where once I saw obstacles. And the best news is that, as author and speaker Wayne Dyer says, "When you change the way you look at things, the things you look at actually begin to change."

3. Change Your Nongrowing Friends

Your friends will either stretch your vision or choke your dreams. Some will inspire you to higher heights. Others will want you to join them on the couch of life where they do their least. Because not everyone wants to see you succeed, you have to make a choice. Are you going to let the people who aren't growing bring you down? Or are you going to move on? This can be a painful and difficult choice, but it can change your life for the better. If you want to be a growing person, you need to spend time with growing people. If you want to be someone who embraces positive change, you need to hang around with positive learners.

There are many roads in life that lead to nowhere. And there are plenty of people who will invite you to join them there. Wise is the person who fortifies his life with the right friendships. Every minute you spend with the wrong people takes away the time you have to spend with the right ones. Change accordingly.

4. Determine to Live Differently than Average People

One of life's important questions is "Who am I?" But even more important is "Who am I becoming?" To answer that question satisfactorily, we must keep one eye on where we are and the other eye on where we will be. Most people don't do that. They have one eye on where they have been and one eye on where they are now. That tells them who they are. (Some people don't even examine themselves *that* much.) However, to know who you are becoming requires you not only to know where you are now but also to know where you're going and how you need to change to get there.

If you are determined to change and to live a life above

and beyond average, know that you need to do things differently as you look ahead. You must...

Think Differently

Successful people are realistic about their problems and find positive ways to approach time. They know that hope isn't a strategy.

Handle Feelings Differently

Successful people don't allow their feelings to determine their behavior. They behave their way into feeling so that they can do what they must to grow and keep moving forward.

Act Differently

Successful people do two things that many other people don't: they initiate action, and they finish what they start. As a result, they form the habit of doing things that unsuccessful people don't.

5. Unlearn What You Know to Learn What You Don't Know

Professional baseball pitcher Satchel Paige said, "It's not what you don't know that hurts you—it's what you do know that just ain't so." That is so true. There are many things that each of us learns are wrong, and we must unlearn them if we want to get better. Unlearning outdated or wrong ways of doing things can be difficult. We tend to lean on what we know, even if it's not the best for us. The secret is to allow yourself to be wrong and to be willing to change for the better. Psychiatrist David Burns says it this way: "Never give up your right to be wrong, because then you will lose the ability to learn new things and move forward with your life."

You've probably heard the statement "If you want something you've never had, you must do something you've never done." It's also true that if you want to become someone you have never been, you must do things you have never done. That means changing what you do every day. If you want to win, you need to change.

12

Benefit from Maturity

The Value of Learning

What do you get if you follow through with all the ideas I've been discussing in this book? You are rewarded with Maturity: The Value of Learning!

When I say *maturity*, I don't mean age. Many people think maturity is a natural result of getting older. When they encounter an immature person, they say, "Give him a few years and he'll mature." Not necessarily. Maturity doesn't always accompany age. Sometimes age comes alone! No, to me a mature person is someone who has learned from losses, has gained wisdom, and possesses a strong emotional and mental stability in the face of life's difficulties.

Author William Saroyan observed, "Good people are good because they've come to wisdom through failure. We get very little wisdom from success, you know." What

Saroyan is describing is this kind of maturity. To some that quality comes at an early age. For others, it never comes.

George Reedy, who was President Lyndon Johnson's press secretary, convinced the president that he should not have any assistants who were younger than forty and who had never suffered any major disappointments in life. Why? Reedy believed they lacked the maturity needed to advise the president. People who haven't overcome major losses are prone to think they are invincible. They start to believe they are better than they really are and are inclined to misuse their power. Everyone who makes a major contribution to life knows what it is to have failures. Maturity is more often developed out of our losses than our wins. But *how* you face those losses really matters. People suffer losses, make mistakes, and endure bad experiences all the time without developing maturity.

The Source of Maturity

If you desire to gain the true value of learning that comes through maturity, then keep in mind the following truths:

1. Maturity Is the Result of Finding the Benefit in the Loss

First, you have to *learn* from your mistakes and losses. That's been the common theme throughout this book. Learning is what investor Warren Buffett has done. People today know him as one of the richest men in the world. This elder statesman is well respected for his financial skill and wisdom, but those qualities have come as a result of learning from his losses. He says, "I make plenty of mistakes and I'll make plenty more mistakes, too. That's part of the game. You've just got to make sure that the right things overcome the wrong ones."

Buffett's mistakes include paying too much for businesses (Conoco Phillips and USAir), buying into sinking businesses (Blue Chip Stamp), missing great opportunities (Capital Cities Broadcasting), hiring poor managers, and running operations himself when he shouldn't have. Yet one of the reasons he is so successful in the face of his losses is that he learns from his mistakes but doesn't dwell on them. I believe the key to being free from the stranglehold of past failures and mistakes is to learn the lesson and forget the details. That brings not only mental advancement but emotional freedom.

Learning from our mistakes is wonderful, but it means little if you don't know how to turn the lesson into a *benefit*. That comes when we take what we've learned and apply it to our future actions. That's what I have tried to do, though it took me a while to learn how to do it. Here are some examples of difficulties I faced, how they affected me emotionally, and how I tried to change my thinking and find the benefit of the experience:

• **When I was over my head writing a Bible commentary:** I felt discouraged, I wanted to quit, and I defined myself as soft. However, I kept working, I got help, and I acquired new ways to learn. Two years later I finished the project. The benefit of the experience: I redefined myself as tenacious. And I never again allowed the challenges of a writing project to prevent me from following through and finishing it.

• **When I had a heart attack:** I realized I had taken my health for granted. I defined myself as undisciplined, and I worried about what the future might hold. But I allowed the experience to change the way I ate and exercised. I began to swim daily. I redefined myself as disciplined in this area for the first time in my life. The benefit: I am living a healthy life every day so that I have additional years with my wife Margaret, our children, and our grandchildren.

• **When my mother died:** I lost the person who gave me unconditional love every day for the first sixty-two years of my life. I was overcome. I felt lost. How many people have someone like that in their lives? And to lose that! But then I realized what a gift she was, and I felt grateful. The benefit: I determined to be that unconditionally loving person in more people's lives.

• **When I lost a million dollars in a bad business decision:** I felt sick because we had to sell some investments to cover the losses, and we couldn't really afford it. I chastised myself because I thought I had been too careless. The benefit: I made some necessary changes in my decision-making process, and I felt much wiser because of the experience.

These key experiences changed me. They taught me lessons, and I benefited when I applied those lessons. When I was young, I mistakenly thought that as I got older and gained experience, I would make fewer mistakes and suffer few losses. That hasn't been true. What I've discovered is that I still make mistakes and face losses, but I learn more quickly from them and am able to move on much more quickly on an emotional level.

If you want to gain the benefits learned from your losses and mistakes, don't allow them to take you captive emotionally. Banker and speaker Herbert V. Prochnow asserted, "The fellow who never makes a mistake takes his orders from one who does." Why? Because the person who advances in his or her career takes risks, fails, learns, and applies the lesson to gain the benefit. Observe any successful person, and you'll see someone who doesn't see a mistake as the enemy. If they have any regrets, they are likely to be like that of actress Tallulah Bankhead, who said, "If I had my life to live over again, I'd make the same mistakes, only sooner."

2. Maturity Is the Result of Learning to Feed the Right Emotions

I believe both positive and negative emotions are contained within each of us. There are people who teach that we should try to eliminate all negative feelings from our lives, but I have never been able to do that. I have tried, but

I found that I simply can't. However, what I *can* do is feed the positive thoughts until they become dominant over the negative ones.

It's said that General George Patton, a fearless warrior of the U.S. Army during World War II, thought of himself as anything but brave. When an official praised his acts of heroism, Patton reportedly responded, "Sir, I am not a brave man. The truth of the matter is I am usually a coward at heart. I have never been in the sound of gunshot or sight of battle in my whole life that I was not afraid. I constantly have sweat on my palms and a lump in my throat." How was someone so afraid able to be so brave? He fed the right emotions. Or as Patton put it himself: "I learned very early in life not to take counsel of my fears."

I try to feed the right emotions within myself by *acting* on the emotion that I want to win. "Do something every day that you don't want to do," advised author Mark Twain. "This is the golden rule for acquiring the habit of doing your duty without pain." Acting on the right emotion will lift you to success. Acting on the wrong emotion will lower you to failure.

I once had lunch with Dom Capers, the successful NFL coach. One of the things he said during our conversation was "Maturity is doing what you are supposed to be doing, when you're supposed to be doing it, no matter how you feel." That's true. The key to success is action. Too often we want to feel our way into acting, when instead we need to act our way into feeling. If we do the right thing, we will eventually feel the right feelings.

3. Maturity Is the Result of Learning to Develop Good Habits

Og Mandino, author of *The Greatest Salesman in the World*, said, "In truth, the only difference between those who have failed and those who have succeeded lies in the difference of their habits." By encouraging the right emotions within us through positive action over a sustained period of time, we can actually form the habit of taking the right action. And that often leads to further positive results. As poet John Dryden put it: "We first make our habits, and then our habits make us."

Good habits require discipline and time to develop. People in high-pressure careers seem to learn this lesson early, or they don't reach the highest levels of success. For example, in professional ice-skating, they call it "staying in your program." When a skater makes a mistake or takes a fall during a routine, he is supposed to immediately get up and jump right back into his program—whether he's competing in the Olympics in front of hawk-eyed judges and millions of television watchers or practicing on his own in the early morning hours. It requires focus and the ability to live in the moment. Why is that important? Because to succeed at that high level, you can't allow a challenge to get you off track. You need to cultivate the habit of executing and following through.

If we want to gain the value of learning, we need to be in the habit of executing at a high level, rain or shine, success or failure, setback or breakthrough. We need to heed the advice of Nobel Peace Prize winner Fridtjof Nansen, who said, "Have you not succeeded? Continue! Have you succeeded? Continue!"

4. Maturity Is the Result of Learning to Sacrifice Today to Succeed Tomorrow

I've touched on this point before, but it bears repeating. There is a definite connection between success and a person's willingness to make sacrifices. In 2012, author Arthur C. Brooks wrote an opinion column for the *Wall Street Journal* that addressed this subject. In it, Brooks states, "People who cannot defer current gratification tend to fail, and sacrifice itself is part of entrepreneurial success." He cites a study from 1972 in which Stanford psychologist Walter Mischel conducted an experiment involving small children and marshmallows. Researchers offered the children a marshmallow but told them they could receive a second one if they waited fifteen minutes without eating the first. Two-thirds of the children failed to wait.

One of the most intriguing things about the study was what researchers discovered later. When they followed up on the children to see how their lives were turning out, they found that the children who had delayed gratification scored on average 210 points higher on the SAT, were less likely to drop out of college, made a higher income, and suffered from fewer drug and alcohol problems.

Brooks goes on to explain some of the implications of the research. He writes,

> But the evidence goes beyond a finding that people who can defer gratification tend to turn out well in general.
>
> When we hear about successful entrepreneurs, it is always as if they had the Midas touch. A pimply college kid cooks up an Internet company during a boring lecture at Harvard, and before lunch he's a billionaire. In real life, that's not how it works. Northwestern University Professor Steven Rogers has shown that the average entrepreneur fails about four times before succeeding.
>
> When asked about their ultimate success, entrepreneurs often talk instead about the importance of their hardships.... When I asked the legendary investment company founder Charles Schwab about the success of the $15 billion corporation that bears his name, he told me the story about taking out a second mortgage on his home just to make payroll in the early years.
>
> Why this emphasis on the struggle? Entrepreneurs know that when they sacrifice, they are learning and improving, exactly what they need to do to earn success through their merits. Every sacrifice

and deferred gratification makes them wiser and better, showing them that they're not getting anything free. When success ultimately comes, they wouldn't trade away the earlier days for anything, even if they felt wretched at the time.[7]

Willingness to sacrifice does not come easily. People naturally tend to adopt behaviors that make them feel good. Everyone likes comfort, pleasure, and entertainment, and they tend to want to reexperience them. If we do this repeatedly, we can become addicted or bored and seek greater pleasures. For some people, this becomes a lifelong pursuit. But there's a problem with that. A person who cannot sacrifice will never belong to himself; he belongs to whatever he was unwilling to give up. If you want to develop maturity and gain the value of learning, you need to learn to give up some things today for greater gains tomorrow.

5. Maturity Is the Result of Learning to Earn Respect for Yourself and Others

The word *esteem* means "to appreciate the worth of, to hold in high regard, to have genuine respect." So *self-esteem* really means "self-respect." That comes from our character. We feel good about ourselves when we make right choices regardless of the circumstances. In fact, if our behavior is positive in the face of negative circumstances, it builds character and self-respect. This comes from inside each of us. And the better prepared we are to face our problems, the greater the maturity and the chance that we can learn and grow.

Author and speaker Brian Tracy says, "Self-esteem is the reputation you have with yourself." If you want it to be solid and lasting, it must be earned and confirmed, day by day. It happens from the inside out. And when it's solid, you know that external forces that come against you aren't going to shake it.

Fred Smith, a mentor of mine for many years, used to tell me, "I don't think God is as interested in our success as He is in our maturity." I believe that. If you desire maturity, even more than you do success, then stay true to who you are to the core, learn from your mistakes, and keep moving forward. That will give you maturity, regardless of your age.

13

Winning Isn't Everything,
but Learning Is

I remember reading a *For Better or Worse* comic strip in which a boy is playing chess with his grandfather. "Oh, no! Not again!" cries the boy. "Grandpa, you always win!"

"What do you want me to do," answers his grandfather, "lose on purpose? You won't learn anything if I do that."

"I don't wanna learn anything," complains the boy. "I just wanna win!"

As well as anything I've ever seen, that captures how most of us feel. We just want to win! But the truth is that winning isn't everything—learning is.

Final Thoughts on Learning

Author Doug Adams said, "You live and learn. At any rate you live." It is possible to win and not learn. However, for people who put winning ahead of learning, life will be difficult. For people who put learning ahead of winning, life will be fulfilling, and they are likely to be rewarded with success as a by-product of their growth.

My purpose in writing this book has been to help you to learn how to learn—from your losses, failures, mistakes, challenges, and bad experiences. I want you to become a continual winner by being a habitual learner. To help you with that, I want to share some final thoughts on learning to help guide you as you go forward.

1. Learning Too Often Decreases as Winning Increases

Complacency: that is the danger any successful person faces. Microsoft founder Bill Gates observed, "Success is a lousy teacher. It makes smart people think they can't lose." It also makes them think they don't need to learn.

The biggest detriment to tomorrow's success is today's success. That problem can manifest itself in many ways. Here are the ones I've observed most often:

• *Been There, Done That:* Some people hit a milestone, and they make it a tombstone. They get bored, lose their curiosity, and disengage. Don't let that happen to you.

• *The Banquet Tour:* When you succeed, people want to hear your story. However, there's a real danger that you can replace doing with speaking.

• *Success Guarantees Success:* Just because you can do one thing well doesn't mean you can do all things well. When you win, maintain your perspective.

• *The Momentum Myth:* People's natural inclination after a win is to take a break. Bad idea. When you're winning, capitalize on the momentum. You'll be able to do things that might otherwise be impossible.

• *One-Hit Wonders:* Have you ever known someone who was successful *once*—and is still living off of it? It's a good idea to *build* off of yesterday; it's a bad idea to *live* off of it.

• *The Entitlement Mind-set:* People who have something that they didn't win for themselves start thinking they are entitled to more. That's why many inherited businesses go *out* of business. To keep winning, you need to stay hungry and keep learning.

• *Playing Not to Lose:* After some people win, they become cautious and defensive. They worry about staying on top. Not wanting to do something stupid, they do something stupid; they focus on not losing instead of winning.

• *The Arrival Plateau:* Some people become so focused on a specific goal that when they hit it they give up, because they believe they've made it. That mind-set has the power to unmake them.

Any one of these wrong attitudes toward winning can turn a person from winner to loser very quickly. If you want to keep learning and growing, you need to stay hungry. Depending on your personality, winning may remove some of your hunger to win again. So instead, keep your hunger to learn. Then no matter whether you win or lose, you'll keep getting better.

2. Learning Is Possible Only When Our Thinking Changes

Have you ever wondered why so many people who win the lottery lose all of their money? This seems to happen continually. One day they're holding a check worth millions, and a few years later they've lost it all. Why is that? The reason they lose their money is that they don't change their thinking. They may receive new money, but they hold on to their same old thinking. It's not what we have that determines our success. It's how we think. If they'd give up their old way of looking at life, then they might hold on to their money.

I've noticed three particular positive thinking patterns of people who are always learning. Adopt them and you will be able to keep changing your thinking in a way to keep you learning:

DON'T LET WHAT YOU KNOW MAKE YOU THINK THAT YOU KNOW IT ALL

Writer and philosopher J. Krishnamurti asserted, "To know is to be ignorant. Not to know is the beginning of wisdom." As you win, and learn and grow, you face a genuine danger of thinking you know it all. Don't let that happen! You simply can't learn what you think you already know.

One of the things that keeps me excited about learning new leadership thoughts is my passion for the subject. I'm still asking other leaders questions about leadership. I'm still exploring. I'm not close to knowing everything about it, and I don't think I ever will be. I don't want to be close. I want to die asking questions and still wanting to learn more. You should be just as passionate about whatever it is you were put on this earth to do. If you can maintain a beginner's mind-set to the end, your thinking will keep changing and you will keep growing.

MAINTAIN A POSITIVE MENTAL ATTITUDE

Writer and thinker G. K. Chesterton said, "How we think when we lose determines how long it will be until we win." I believe a key part of the right kind of thinking comes from remaining positive. How do you do that? By continually feeding positive thoughts to your mind by reading positive books, collecting positive quotes, and listening to positive messages. When you do that, you supply your thinking with plenty of positive material, and you keep your mind focused on things that will encourage you.

When negative ideas and discouraging thoughts want to creep in and make you negative, you will have already created a barrier to them. Think positively long enough, and not only will your positive thoughts be stronger than your negative ones, they will be more comfortable, too.

Maintaining a consistently positive mental attitude will be your greatest ally in growing and learning. If you can remain positive, then even when things go wrong, you won't break a sweat. Your attitude will be, *The worst thing that could happen to me today could lead to the best thing that happens today.*

Embrace Creativity in Every Situation

Creativity is the ability to free yourself from imaginary boundaries, to see new relationships, and to explore options so that you can accomplish more things of value. What holds people back from their potential is all the imaginary boundaries they have allowed to imprison their thinking and doing. Wonderful, workable options are the rewards for becoming more creative. Greater learning comes from better thinking. That requires us to change.

3. Real Learning Is Defined as a Change in Behavior

The greatest gap in life is the one between knowing and doing. I can't count the number of people I've met who *know* what they are supposed to do yet don't take action on it. Sometimes it's due to fear. Other times to laziness. Other times to emotional dysfunction. The problem is that knowing what to do and *not* doing it is no better than not knowing what to do. It ends in the same result. Stagnation. You haven't really learned something until you've lived it. Or as poet Ralph Waldo Emerson said, "Life is a succession of lessons which must be lived to be understood."

My friend Dave Ramsey, a financial expert who writes books, teaches seminars, and hosts a syndicated radio show, places a very high premium on action when he teaches and counsels people about money and finances. During a recent interview he pointed out, "What I found is that personal finance is 80 percent behavior. Everybody tries to fix financial problems with math. But it's not a math problem, and it's not a knowledge problem. It's a behavior problem. The problem with my money is the idiot I shave with every morning. If I can get that guy in the mirror to behave, he can be skinny and rich. It's not magic."[8] That's true. Turning learning into changed behavior isn't magic. But it is magical. It can change your life.

4. Continual Success Is a Result of Continually Failing and Learning

Chicago teacher Marva Collins says, "If you can't make a mistake, you can't make anything." How true. If you want to be successful, you must be willing to fail, and you must be intent on learning from those failures. If we are willing to repeat this fail-and-learn process, we become stronger and better than we were before.

In his book *Life's Greatest Lessons*, Hal Urban describes

this process. He calls it "Strong at the Broken Places."
Urban writes,

> Near the end of *A Farewell to Arms*, Ernest Heming-
> way's famous novel about World War I, he wrote,
> "The world breaks everyone and afterward many are
> strong at the broken places." The world does, indeed,
> break everyone, and usually not just once. But as a
> broken bone becomes even stronger when it heals, so
> do we. It all depends on our attitude and our choices.
> We can become stronger at our broken places if
> we choose to learn from our mistakes, correct our
> course, and try again. Our failures in life, as painful
> as they are, can be our most valuable learning expe-
> riences and our greatest source of renewed strength.
> As General George S. Patton said, "Success is how
> high you bounce after you hit bottom."[9]

My hope for you is that you will bounce high—and keep
bouncing. With each successive bounce back, you'll be able
to go higher and farther. That's what success in life is: the
learned ability to keep bouncing back. As author and entre-
preneur Joseph Sugarman says, "If you're willing to accept
failure and learn from it, if you're willing to consider failure as a blessing in disguise and bounce back, you've got
the potential of harnessing one of the most powerful success forces."

Focus and Risk as You Win, Lose, and Learn

As you move forward in life and work to achieve success, remember that progress requires risk, leads to failure, and provides many learning opportunities. Anytime you try something new, you must risk. That's just a part of learning. But there's an art to managing that risk, and it comes from successfully coordinating the two zones for success that you have in your life: your strength zone, where you do your best work; and your comfort zone, where you feel safe.

To maximize your success, you must make the most of your successes and failures. To do that, you need to get in your strength zone but get out of your comfort zone. Take a look at how this works:

STRENGTH ZONE	COMFORT ZONE	RESULT
Outside Your Strength Zone	Outside Your Comfort Zone	Poor Performance— Winning Is Impossible
Outside Your Strength Zone	Inside Your Comfort Zone	Mediocre Performance— Winning Is Impossible
Inside Your Strength Zone	Inside Your Comfort Zone	Good Performance— Winning Is Possible
Inside Your Strength Zone	Outside Your Comfort Zone	Great Performance— Winning Is Continual

Traditional wisdom and, frankly, the focus of most education, is to shore up your weaknesses. But that's not where you will do your best work. People don't succeed if they focus their time and effort outside of their strength zone. You have to major in your strengths. That's where your productivity resides. The recent work of the Gallup organization bears this out and is discussed extensively in the Strengths Finder books and testing instruments they've published.

While it's true that your greatest successes will be in your strength zone, it's also true that your best failures will occur there. Why do I say that? Because you'll recover the fastest and learn the most where your talent and skills are strongest. For example, one of my greatest strengths is communication. Let's say I try something new onstage when I'm speaking to an audience, and it fails miserably. I will probably be able to figure out what went wrong very quickly. I might even be able to diagnose the problem and make the necessary adjustments while I'm still onstage speaking. And because I'm working in my strength, I'll understand the problem and won't repeat what I did wrong.

In contrast, let's say I have a problem with my car. I'm driving down the road and it quits on me. The only thing I know how to do in that situation is check the fuel gauge. If that's not the problem, I have absolutely no chance of figuring out how to fix it. The only thing I can do in that situation is call my mechanic. And even if he explains *exactly* what was wrong, there won't be anything I can do about it if it happens again in the future. Why? Because it's totally out of my strength zone.

I'm sure the process is similar for you. If you're outside of your strength zone, a problem is a mystery. If you're in your strength zone, a problem is a challenge, a learning experience, and a road to improvement. That's why you need to get out of your comfort zone by taking risks while working in your strength zone. When you take risks, you learn things faster than the people who don't take risks. You experiment. You learn more about what works and what doesn't. You overcome obstacles more quickly than the people who play it safe and are able to build on those experiences.

Keep Climbing

The greatest education you ever receive will come from taking risks in your area of strength. Risk taking without ability leads to increased frustration and continual failure. Risk taking with ability leads to increased learning and success.

I don't know what your personal Mount Everest is—what you were put on this earth to do. Everybody has one. But I do know this: win or lose, you need to try to reach the summit. If you don't, you will always regret it. As you get older, you will find that you become more disappointed by the things you didn't attempt than by the ones you tried and failed to achieve. And here's the best news. Every step of the way there's something to learn. You are enrolled in a full-time informal school called life. In it, there are no mistakes, only lessons. Growth is a process of trial and error, experimentation and improvement. The failed experiments are as much of that process as the ones that work.

The lessons you have the opportunity to learn will be presented to you in various forms. Fail to learn the lesson and you get stuck, unable to move forward. Learn the lesson and you get to move forward and on to the next one. And if you do it right, the process never ends.

There is no part of life that doesn't contain lessons. If you're alive, that means you still have opportunities ahead of you to learn. You just have to be willing to tackle them. You have all the tools and resources you need. The choice is yours. Others will give you advice. Some may even help you. But you have to take the test of life yourself. Sometimes you will win. Sometimes you will lose. But every time you will have the opportunity to ask yourself, "What did I learn?" If you always have an answer to that question, then you will go far. You will enjoy the journey. And you will have learned how successful people win.

Notes

1. Charlotte Foltz Jones, *Mistakes That Worked* (New York: Double-day, 1991), introduction.
2. Patricia Sellers, "So You Fail. Now Bounce Back!" CNNMoney, May 1, 1995, http://money.cnn.com/magazines/fortune/fortune_archive/1995/05/01/202473/index.htm, accessed August 27, 2012.
3. Frances Cole Jones, *The Wow Factor: The 33 Things You Must (and Must Not) Do to Guarantee Your Edge in Today's Business World* (New York: Ballantine Books, 2009), 30–31.
4. Kevin Kelly, "The Speed of Information," *The Technium* (blog), February 20, 2006, http://www.kk.org/thetechnium/archives/2006/02/the_speed_of_in.php, accessed August 29, 2012.
5. Jonathan Sacks, *The Dignity of Difference: How to Avoid the Clash of Civilizations* (New York: Continuum, 2002), 206.
6. Robert H. Schuller, *Tough Times Never Last, But Tough People Do!* (New York: Bantam Books, 1984), 73.
7. Arthur C. Brooks, "Obama's Budget Flunks the Marshmallow Test," *Wall Street Journal*, February 24, 2012, http://online.wsj.com/article/SB10001424052970204880404577229220571408412.html, accessed October 8, 2012.
8. "Mentors: Dave Ramsey," *Success*, September–October 2006, 40.
9. Hal Urban, *Life's Greatest Lessons: 20 Things That Matter* (New York: Fireside, 2003), 156.

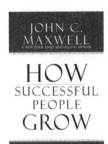